Hogg, G   MARKET TOWNS
              OF ENGLAND.

9412   O.S. 942
             864.

MARKET TOWNS
OF ENGLAND

Books by the same author

Market Towns of England

by GARRY HOGG

DAVID & CHARLES
NEWTON ABBOT LONDON NORTH POMFRET (VT) VANCOUVER

0 7153   6798 6

Set in 12 on 13 point Plantin
and printed in Great Britain
by Compton Printing Limited, Aylesbury
for David & Charles (Holdings) Limited
South Devon House Newton Abbot Devon

Published in the United States of America
by David & Charles Inc   North Pomfret
Vermont 05053 USA

Published in Canada by Douglas David &
Charles Limited   3645 McKechnie Drive
West Vancouver BC

Contents

Author's Foreword

Part way between the 'show villages' of England such as Amberley and Arkesden, Castle Combe and Finchingfield, Lavenham, Grasmere and Widecombe-in-the-Moor at one end of the spectrum, and the splendour and antiquity of our cathedral cities such as Durham and Ely, Canterbury and York, Lincoln and Wells, are to be found the country market towns of England. Though these are so widely distributed, paradoxically it may be said that they constitute the true heart of England. Their pulse was beating strongly, driving England's blood-stream through its veins and bringing life to its scattered small communities long before the clamour of the weaving-sheds of Lancashire and Yorkshire's cotton and wool manufactories broke upon the ear; long before the thudding trip-hammers of the Black Country's ironfoundries and steelworks became an inescapable background to everyday life; long before the decibel-count of the Tyneside shipyard riveters rose to its almost unbearable level.

These market towns became the nuclei of the small communities that established themselves where fresh water flowed and became hamlets of a hundred souls, villages of several hundreds and more. For a long while they were self-contained and self-supporting; but inevitably some expanded, assuming for one reason or another an importance greater than their immediate neighbours', and came to be recognised as the focal points for the smaller communities scattered about the whole region. Here the farmer's wife could bring her poultry, eggs and butter; the cottager the gloves or shawls she had made beneath her own roof; selling or bartering of essential commodities could be carried on to mutual advantage; the farmer could buy and sell cattle and grain, the wool merchant could trade in fleeces or yarn or the finished product. The story of the development of trading in this country, as elsewhere, is packed with interest; it is largely recorded in the market towns of England.

Often their very names bespeak their origin and function: Market Harborough, Market Deeping, Market Bosworth and Market Drayton. Less obviously, many names contain the word 'Chipping', which has the same connotation: Chipping Campden, Chipping Norton, Chipping Sodbury and Chipping Warden. (A variant of the word appears in London's Cheapside and Eastcheap.) In by far the greatest number of instances there is no hint of the importance of the town actually explicit in the name it bears.

There is, however, a certain quality about a market town that can be swiftly sensed. It is compounded of various elements, which together create what may be called its ambience. The town lies, perhaps, in the heart of rolling agricultural country and, as you approach it, you note the flocks of sheep grazing on the wolds; the town has prospered from centuries of sheep rearing and wool production. Or the town lies in the heart of some lush vale where the water meadows are grazed by sleek cattle; dairy-farming and cattle-breeding, the buying and selling of butter and milk as well as beasts, will have been the staple industry of the town, maybe for centuries past. And so on.

In such towns, for all that developers and town-planners can do, there is almost invariably an unmistakable market place. Even if the site of the original market has perforce been moved to the outskirts, the names Market Place or Square will have been retained. It is in these market places that the prime feature of almost all market towns will be found: the market hall, market house, or market cross. Many of these date back to medieval times and are the treasured possession of the townsfolk; some of them are newer buildings erected on the site of the original buildings, perhaps destroyed by fire several centuries ago but immediately rebuilt because of their importance.

Many of these market halls – as will be seen in the illustrations in this book – are buildings of beauty and distinction quite apart from their functional aspect; some are regarded as important enough to have had Preservation Orders laid upon them and are listed as Ancient Monuments by the Department of the Environment. Though they are of course less impressive than our cathedrals and many of our stately homes, they nevertheless have a beauty and integrity that is wholly their own. In their massive stonework, as at Chipping Campden, Tetbury or Ross-on-Wye, or in their splendid half-timbering, as at Ledbury, Thaxted or Market Harborough, they epitomise the essence of the life that has for centuries revolved about and within them.

Not all of them are actually houses, with a stone or oak-pillared ground floor in which the trading was carried on and an upper floor where the town authorities assembled to administer its affairs and dispense justice. Sometimes – as at Oakham, Malmesbury or Dunster – the structure is a more or less ornate cross, of stone or timber or both, lightly or ornately roofed: in essence a central pillar with tiers of well-worn steps on which the traders struck their bargains beneath a spreading roof that sheltered them from inclement weather.

A number of these market towns were first granted market charters seven or eight centuries ago; Abingdon's market is recorded in the Domesday Book, which was compiled in 1086. Sometimes, though the market house, hall or cross survives, the market itself has shifted to some other centre. Newer towns have established and developed markets of their own, along less specialised lines than, say, wool, cattle, horses, farm produce: Newton Abbot is an example of this, with a regular market that attracts customers from a very wide area indeed. Some towns have had their former open markets totally enclosed, for the convenience of traders and customers alike; others retain the old, and hence more picturesque, tradition of the open market.

In the following pages, fifty-one of these country towns, with the emphasis very much on their market aspect, have been picked, from thirty counties, ranging from Northumbria to the Duchy of Cornwall, from East Anglia and Kent to the Welsh border. Any one of the towns selected could have been matched by others from the same county. Most of them date back to the Middle Ages; some, like Beverley and Evesham and Bury St Edmunds, owe their birth and growth to the proximity of a priory or abbey. At the Dissolution of the Monasteries these largely ceased to exist, but the towns that had grown up around them happily survived, and do so to this day.

A few of the choices in this book may strike the reader as odd. Though they are country towns they are not, in the strict sense of the term, market towns; nor do they date back as far in time as the majority. Nevertheless, for one reason or another, they merit inclusion. Blandford Forum, for example: though the unique second part of its name suggests great antiquity and Roman associations, it is less than three centuries old, for the greater part of it was destroyed by fire in the mid-eighteenth century. Royal Leamington Spa is another. A century and a half ago it was a mere village; it is now, and for a very different reason, a thriving and elegant country town – a 'new town' at least in contrast with the medieval towns that occupy most of these pages, if less new than Crawley, Basildon and Milton Keynes.

Is not a great part of the pleasure of exploring this country derived from the element of surprise and contrast, as well as seeing for the first time a place hitherto only known about at second hand? Certainly I believe this to be the case; I hope that the point, among so many others, will be appreciated as these pages of pictures and accompanying text are being turned.

Groombridge, Sussex. G.H.

Berkshire

ABINGDON

Until 1867 this was the County Town, with a known history dating back to Saxon times. Quite recently, the Council for British Archaeology listed some three hundred towns that particularly merited preservation; of these, fifty were short-listed for special mention 'because their centres are so splendid and precious that ultimate responsibility for them should be a national concern'. One of the fifty was Abingdon.

Throughout some thirteen centuries of active life, its centre, the 'burgh', or as it was known till recently, the 'Bury', has been its market place. The existence of a market here is recorded in the Domesday Book reference, in AD 1086, to 'Ten Traders before the Gates of the Church'; the market received its official Charter in 1328, 'To be Held on Monday'; it is so held to this day, more than six centuries later.

The Market Place is dominated by the gateway of the ancient Benedictine Abbey (lower picture), flanked by the twelfth-century St Nicholas Church and the St John's Hospital, now the Guildhall. Its chief feature, however, is the seventeenth-century Market (or County) Hall, erected by Sir Christopher Wren's Master-Builder on the site of the Market Hall of 1327. No less eminent an authority than Sir Nikolaus Pevsner has written: 'Of the free-standing town halls of England with open ground floors, this is the grandest.' During the centuries its cellars have served as warehouses; its open-sided, arcaded ground floor as a covered market; its spacious upper floor as Sessions Hall. From the balustraded roof, on special occasions, buns are still thrown to the populace, as they have been ever since the reign of George IV.

When the town was a centre of the wool and cloth trade, the fifteenth-century Fraternity of the Holy Cross built the beautiful composite bridge over the Thames. The same organisation was responsible for the Long Alley Almshouses (upper picture) adjoining St Helen's Church, designed to accommodate 'Thirteen Poore, Sick and Impotent Men and Women'; they are still permanently occupied. From the Market Place, East St Helen Street, flanked by eighteenth-century red brick buildings of distinction, leads down to them. Ock Street is the setting for the annual two-day Michaelmas Fair, originally a 'Hiring Fair', followed by the curiously named 'Runaway Fair' in which discontented employees had the chance to cancel their twelve-month contracts. So, the range here is from the medieval, by way of markets, to modern shopping precinct.

AYLESBURY

The town was of importance in Anglo-Saxon times; it is on record that the Saxons drove the Britons from this pleasant site in the great Vale that extends between Bedfordshire and Oxfordshire in AD 571; the Danes drove out the Saxons in 921. Coins were minted here from the tenth century into Norman times; Assizes were long held here and Knights elected in the thirteenth and fourteenth centuries. Aylesbury Market – corn, cattle, sheep and pigs and of course the famous ducklings – dates back to 1554, when Queen Mary granted the town its Borough Charter.

The Market Square was, and remains, the focal point of the town (upper picture), though the cattle market has now found a new site. The sloping square is dominated by a clock tower and, on its upper slope, by a fine statue to the great John Hampden, and another to Disraeli. Some idea of its importance as a meeting-place for traders generally is gained from the presence of so many fine hotels overlooking it. Notable among these is the splendid fifteenth-century *King's Head*. It was originally the guest house of a monastery and its cobbled courtyard is entered by a medieval gateway. History is enshrined here: a leaded window bears the arms of Henry VI and Queen Margaret of Anjou, and also those of the Prince Edward who died at the Battle of Tewkesbury. You may see also the so-called 'Cromwell's Chair', reputedly used by him when he stayed here on his return from the Battle of Worcester. Oddly, the town was a base for both Royalists and Roundheads at different periods. Here too is the comparatively rare so-called 'Act of Parliament Clock' (lower picture).

Turn off the Market Square and search among the narrow side streets. You will come to the interesting *Dark Lantern Inn*; to the much later, eighteenth-century Prebendal House, once the home of the noted satirist, John Wilkes MP, in Parson's Fee. Here too is the sixteenth-century St Osyth, the old Prebendal Farm; also some interesting timber-framed houses, including the ancient Clergy House. But, as so often, the oldest building of all is the church. St Mary's dates mainly from the thirteenth century but occupies a sacred site known six centuries earlier. It offers a wealth of records covering the centuries, including a fluted Norman font and an alabaster memorial to Lady Lee who died in 1584 with the request that red flowers should be placed by her tomb 'in perpetuity'; the request is dutifully fulfilled to this day.

BARNARD CASTLE

An aerial view would show this town as laid out in a loop on a steepish slope upwards from the River Tees, which must be crossed by its ancient bridge beneath the cliff on which are the ruins of the castle (lower picture) first built by Guy de Bailleul before 1100 and rebuilt in 1150 by his nephew Bernard, whose name and fame the town commemorates. The fourteenth-century Round Tower dominates all else, and influenced Scott in writing his poem, *Rokeby*. The town grew up and away from the castle: a market town of much importance in the north and notable especially for its shoe-thread making, harness and rope-making and weaving of cloth. A number of houses, notably in Thorngate, reveal long upper-storey windows customary in those used by loom workers in their weaving-lofts in many parts of the country, from these northern counties down to Kent.

The Market Place is on a slope, dominated by the Parish Church of St Mary. Appropriately for a town so named, it has fifteenth-century battlements, but its South Porch dates back to late Norman times. Originally it had that comparatively rare feature, a detached tower, but the present tower is comparatively modern, in strong contrast to the successive centuries' work so evident in the main structure.

It overlooks the mid-eighteenth-century Market Hall (upper picture). This is octagonal in shape and three-tiered. A number of Doric-style columns, all different in height as they stand on a slope, support a lean-to tiled roof so that the market stall-holders selling dairy and other produce were at once sheltered and accessible. Heavy pillars supporting the central portion were formerly linked to constitute the town's gaol and steps led to the first floor, where the town's affairs were ordered and records kept. The uppermost tier is a bell-turret with a weather-vane in which you can see two holes, pierced by shots from rival marksmen firing from the door of an inn a hundred yards distant, in 1804. They certainly were not the worse for drink!

Every small street here has its historic buildings, each with its own story: Galgate, for instance; Horsemarket; The Bank; Priory Yard— relic, probably, of an Augustinian friary. Much more modern, however, is the famous Bowes Museum, built in 1869 in French Renaissance style for private occupation and subsequently acquired by the County Council; many connoisseurs consider it to be one of the most outstanding museums to be found outside London and the half-dozen major cities.

BARNSTAPLE

Set on the banks of the River Taw at its junction with the Yeo, this claims to be the oldest borough, not merely in Devon but in all England. It was a Saxon stronghold, and King Alfred's grandson, King Athelstan, granted it a Charter in AD 930, with the right to hold a market and annual fairs; the mint he also established there produced coins for centuries afterwards. The chief market, known universally as the Pannier Market, thrives to this day; it is now held in an unusually impressive nineteenth-century vaulted building linked to the Guildhall, and in it Devon clotted cream, eggs, fruit, flowers and vegetables are sold on innumerable stalls amid a throng of local customers and visitors from far and wide to this, the chief market town in North Devon. There is also the annual three-day Fair, held in September, thanks to a special charter granted to the borough in medieval times. It is officially opened, with elaborate ceremonial, in the Guildhall; privileged persons imbibe spiced ale from silver loving-cups, ale brewed by the Senior Beadle from a treasured Elizabethan recipe. Other West Country mayors gather here in strength to participate in the ceremony.

Though much of this ancient ship-building town (it supplied five ships for Drake's defeat of the Spanish Armada) has been modernised, there remains plenty of medievalism. The fourteenth-century Parish Church of St Peter, for instance, with its extraordinary twisted broach spire, reminiscent of that at Chesterfield; the Alice Horwood School, endowed in 1659 'for 20 Poore Children for Ever'; the fourteenth-century Chapel of St Anne, built as a 'charnel chapel', later used as a grammar school and now a museum of antiquities; the very unusual Butchers Row (lower picture), an arcade of small, identical shops facing the Pannier Market; the charming little Queen Anne's Walk, laid out in 1609 and rebuilt a century later as the Merchants Exchange, where you may see the curious and ancient 'Tome Stone' on which money was laid as merchants sealed their bargains. The majority of Barnstaple's inhabitants, however, certainly rate foremost among their treasures the magnificent Long Bridge (upper picture) that spans the Taw, linking The Square with Sticklepath. It possesses no fewer than sixteen arches. The earliest historical records to it date back to 1273, though the structure you see today, after successive stages of restoration and necessary widening, dates back only to about 1437.

BEVERLEY

This is another of the many towns that, like Evesham and Malmesbury, grew up round a very ancient monastic settlement: the original monastery and church were established here in the seventh century. With its vast surrounding acreage of pasture land, it quickly became an agricultural centre. Its Market Cross (lower picture), dating from 1714 but undoubtedly replacing a much older one, is a reminder of this: it is the focal point of the centuries-old Saturday Market. It is an open, octagonal structure erected on 8 pillars supporting a domed roof with urn-like pinnacles and rising to a most graceful lantern turret and weather-vane.

The Gothic minster (upper picture), the fourth church to be built on this site, is regarded by experts as the most beautiful church in all England that is below cathedral status; it shows work of the thirteenth, fourteenth and fifteenth centuries at its best, notably the canopy of the famous Percy Shrine. The minster itself is remarkable for its very unusual dual-cruciform style of building, and is matched, if on a just less impressive scale, by the Church of St Mary not far away, one of the finest of all our parish churches. It is interesting particularly in that it was originally the chapel-of-ease to the minster but, as the affluence of the agriculturalists, merchants and traders grew, came to be especially associated with them. Its foundations were laid in the early twelfth century and it continued to be enlarged and beautified for no less than four hundred years. Not far from it is the gateway known as North Bar Within, where there are many examples of Georgian architecture to be seen, as well as some medieval half-timbering. Hengate is another treasure.

Like King's Lynn, Norfolk, Beverley is remarkable for having not one but two separate market places. The Wednesday Market was granted its Charter by Elizabeth I 'for all manner of cattle and chattels there to be bought and sold'. It has flourished ever since, for this remains a busy place, close to the Humber and with long-established trade up and down the estuary to Kingston upon Hull and thence across the North Sea to the scattered markets of Europe. A reminder of this may be seen in the Guildhall, which was erected in the seventeenth century: always a sign that guilds of craftsmen – and these include tanners and rope-makers – and merchants were recognised and cherished; essential components of any true market town.

BLANDFORD FORUM

The town has a double claim to call itself unique. Firstly, it is the only town in England to have the word *Forum* in its name; secondly, it is the only town to have been built in the eighteenth century. This claim may seem contradictory, for *forum* is the Romans' word for a place of assembly, including a market, which suggests true antiquity; in fact, there was a market here as long ago as 1225, held on Saturdays. But on 4 June 1731, at two o'clock in the afternoon, fire broke out in a tallow-chandler's shop; within a matter of hours, four hundred of the little town's timber and thatched buildings were alight, all the local fire-fighting equipment was out of action and, with the exception of a very few stone-roofed buildings, the whole town was destroyed and countless lives lost. But, like the Marques de Pombal after the earthquake and fire in Lisbon in 1755, and our own Christopher Wren who rebuilt London in 1666, two local architects, John and William Bastard, set to and rebuilt the town in the largely Georgian red brick and stone that you see today. Blandford is, in fact, the 'Shottesford Forum' of Hardy's Wessex novels.

Ryves Almshouses, of 1682, with the rare tulip tree in their garden, survived the fire, thanks to their stone roofs; so did The Old House, occupied by the doctor in the year of the fire, and Dale House, which dates from 1689. But what constitutes the town today is almost entirely the work of the Bastard brothers. An example of their building style is the house occupied by John Bastard, known today as Electric House (lower picture). They laid out the whole town anew, giving it a notably fine market place; they built the impressive Town Hall (upper picture), on the left of the Corn Exchange; they rebuilt the Parish Church of SS Peter and Paul, near which a portico in classic style commemorates 'God's Dreadful Visitation by Fire' when, according to contemporary observers, 'the lead melted, the stone split and flew; nay, so fervent and irresistible was the heat that the bells dissolved and ran down in streams'.

Hard to believe that so hideous a disaster could ever have struck so gracious a little town as Blandford Forum is today, for an air of prosperity, of serenity, prevails there. The placid Stour glides past its southern flanks; but here again is a reminder of harshness: an iron plaque on the bridge, matched elsewhere in the county, gives warning that 'Any Person Wilfully Injuring Any Part of the County Bridge Will Be Guilty of a Felony and Upon Conviction Liable to be Transported for Life'.

BOSTON

The name is believed to be a corruption of 'St Botolph's Tun', the saint having founded a monastery here in AD 654, fifty years after St Augustine's arrival in Kent. The Church of St Botolph (upper picture) with its 'Stump', one of eighty dedicated to the saint, is the second largest of our parish churches; built on the site of the original church, its splendour and richness of ornamentation testify to the wealth and piety of the medieval wool traders who built it. From its octagonal tower a beacon light shone out for the benefit of seamen and fenlanders alike, its beam visible for twenty miles. It rises to 272ft 6in; 365 steps lead up to it, and the church has 12 pillars, 52 windows, 7 doors, 24 steps to the library and 60 to the roof-loft, suggesting a link between calendar and time and the church.

In the Middle Ages the town had a harbour and developed a busy trade with the continent, notably the Low Countries; something of the influence of Low Countries' architecture catches the eye here and there. By the end of the eighteenth century the harbour had silted up and this ceased to be England's principal east coast port. But though trade diminished, what it had resulted in remains to this day. There is, for instance, the Guildhall, used from 1545 onwards and restored with American aid in 1911; it now serves as a most interesting local museum, with much fifteenth-century glass, a minstrels' gallery, chimneys with spits operated by the mounting heat from the huge fireplaces, and much else. Eighteenth-century Fydell House is dedicated to the use of Americans, and is in strong contrast with the medieval Blackfriars, once part of a Dominican friary and now, happily, in use as a Repertory Theatre.

On 4 July every year (America's Thanksgiving Day) the Stars and Stripes are flown from masts and windows, a reminder of the close link with the United States. From near Boston there sailed the Pilgrim Fathers, after much trouble and persecution (cells in which they were incarcerated may be seen in the Guildhall); they landed in America and founded Boston, Massachusetts – closest of links. A model of the *Mayflower* (lower picture) is one of several interesting reminders and records, to be found in the Parish Church of St Botolph. In Trinity Church, Boston, across the Atlantic, there may be seen tracery taken from one of St Botolph's Perpendicular-style chancel windows, again a close, even intimate, link between towns sharing their name.

BURFORD

This is one of the most beautiful of the larger townships in the eastern half of the Cotswolds, a 'symphony in grey-gold limestone', every building an eye-catching treasure. There is good reason for this: though its origin goes back to the seventh-century Kingdom of Mercia, on whose edge it stood, it began really to flourish when William the Conqueror made it over as a 'Manor' to Bishop Odo of Bayeux; soon afterwards it was granted a 'Guild Merchant' – the first English town to be so honoured; this included the right of a Saturday Market and an annual Midsummer Fair during the Feast of St John the Baptist, which is known far and wide, charmingly, as 'Cherry Fair'.

Its glory lies in the beauty of the buildings large and small that line both sides of the main street (upper picture), sloping down to the three-arched bridge over the Windrush where Elizabeth I presented Burford (the burgh-at-the-ford) with a purse of '20 Golden Angels'. The distinction of many of these buildings is due to the fact that they were designed by a local quarry owner who worked on St Paul's for Sir Christopher Wren and later employed many of Wren's own masons to build them. Many, however, are much older. For example, a house at the top of The Hill owned by a man named Huntley whose wife made *bis-coctum* – twice-baked – cakes, later the biscuits of Huntley & Palmer. Another is The Tolsey, originally a timber-framed chamber on eight octagonal columns where market and other tolls were collected; in its restored form it is now the Council Chamber, with twin gables, bay windows, clock and bell. Early sixteenth-century, it also houses a small museum. Other beautiful buildings include *The Bull* (formerly *The Bear*), noteworthy for its admixture of warm brick and stone. Some other buildings have Georgian façades superimposed upon older fabric, yet they accord well with the general display of stonework. In the immediate district, happily, there are still craftsmen who can handle the local stone, whether dry-walling (lower picture) or in full-scale building.

Overlooking the Windrush is the parish church, its Norman tower topped by a slender spire. Bullet marks from a Cromwellian firing squad may be detected on an outer wall; on the lead of the font are scratched the words: 'Anthony Sedley 1649 prisner': he and 350 others were imprisoned there. Near by are the old almshouses. The town's wealth grew, not from wool but from the ancillary trades: dyers, clothiers, tailors, weavers, tanners, and also slaters and 'spicers' – or grocers.

BURY ST EDMUNDS

The origins of this town are lost in the turmoil of the Anglo-Saxon period. The body of King Edmund, martyred by the Vikings in 869 AD, was buried in the grounds of the early eleventh-century monastery, to which King Canute gave the status of abbey: hence the name of this charming cathedral-cum-market town, the 'burgh', or borough, of St Edmund. It was Abbot Baldwin who, one year before the Norman invasion, laid out the town as you see it today; it is a chess-board pattern of narrow streets to the west of the abbey grounds and represents one of the earliest examples of town planning in England. Stand with your back to the Abbey Gateway, dated 1327, and you look across the wide open Angel Hill, with Angel Corner (opposite) on your right; this houses the justifiably famous Gershom Parkinton Memorial Collection of clocks and watches. Abbeygate Street climbs away from where you stand.

It leads to Cornhill, with the impressive Market Cross (in fact an Adam-designed building which now houses an interesting Art Gallery); near by is the curiously-known Moyses Hall, which started life in the twelfth century as a pair of Norman dwellings and now serves appropriately as a museum. Not far away is Cupola House, an impressive seventeenth-century three-storey building with mullioned windows and a true cupola surmounting its lofty roof; it was once the home of Thomas Macro, Burgess and Chief Magistrate. Turn left, and you come to the Guildhall, whose thirteenth-century central porch has been designated an Ancient Monument. Beyond again, in Westgate Street, is the Theatre Royal, the third oldest theatre in England and the sole surviving Regency one. Happily, it is thriving today.

Inevitably you return to Angel Hill and Crown Street, flanking the ancient abbey buildings whose remains are scattered through the Gardens. Here is the famous *Angel Hotel,* known to all who have read *The Pickwick Papers;* its vaults date from the thirteenth century. Having looked again, and closely, at the Abbey Gateway, look next at the exquisite Notyngham Porch of fifteenth-century St Mary's Church, and particularly at its carved 'angel roof': you will find the 'missing angel's hand' in the chancel. Here Mary Tudor was buried, sister of Henry VIII, on whose Edict of Dissolution this Benedictine abbey ceased to exist. Much of the medieval town was destroyed in a great fire in 1608; this explains why there is so much late seventeenth and eighteenth-century architecture: a note of elegance here prevails.

CHICHESTER

As the latter part of the name suggests, this was originally a Roman town: a base was quickly established here when they landed in AD 43 and you can still see part of the massive wall and bastion, to the south of the cathedral (like Lichfield, Chichester is a small cathedral city); and at Fishbourne, near by, are the remains of the largest Roman building in all England.

It is also partly Saxon in origin, for Aella, first of the Saxon kings, gave the Roman *castra* to his son, Cissa: hence the name Chichester. Save possibly in Chester, the Roman layout of a town is nowhere better seen than here. Four main streets, named after the four compass-points, radiate from the focal point, the Market Cross. This is regarded by connoisseurs as the finest surviving cross of the kind in England, surpassing that of Malmesbury. It is medieval, a gift to the town by Bishop Story in the fifteenth century to serve countryfolk coming in to sell their wares. The octagonal structure consists of ornate arches flanked by flying buttresses that support a 50ft cupola. Bishops' mitres, cinquefoiled heads, carved bosses and rich finials, all in Caen stone, lend a grace to this most beautiful structure.

Today, the chief impression (apart from the cathedral and Market Cross) is of a Georgian town full of elegant, well-windowed buildings. They are to be seen at their best in a small street called Little London, and the area on the opposite side of East Street, The Pallants. There is evidence of occupation of the site for nineteen centuries: the Roman walls and bastions; the Chantry, off Canon Lane, originating in the thirteenth century; the Hospital of the Blessed Mary, of the same century, both rest home for the aged and a chapel; the charming cul-de-sac named Vicar's Close (upper picture). The cathedral was founded in the early twelfth century and added to at intervals; its 277ft spire, erected in the fourteenth century, was destroyed in a storm a century ago, but rebuilt exactly as it had originally been. But we come to modern times when we see in the chancel John Piper's superbly vivid tapestry, though it hangs from a sixteenth-century carved screen. By no means the least important modern feature in the town is the Festival Theatre (lower picture), opened in 1962. It is open-plan, with steeply-tiered seats, not one of which is more than sixty-six feet from the stage; there is nothing comparable with this theatre in all England.

Gloucestershire

CHIPPING CAMPDEN

The 'Chipping' in the name, as with Chipping Norton, Chipping Barnet, Cheapside, and Chipping Ongar and elsewhere, indicates that the original function of the town was that of a market; here it is epitomised in the beautiful seventeenth-century stoned-arched and tile-roofed Market Hall (lower picture), though this is only one of the innumerable fine buildings constructed of the incomparable oolitic limestone for which the Cotswolds are famous. The town as a whole is evidence of the prosperity of the wool merchants of the fourteenth and fifteenth centuries. Outstanding among its beautiful buildings is the house of William Grevel, which dates from 1380 and is noteworthy especially for the noble two-storeyed and gabled bay window. Fine brass memorials to him and his wife are set in the stone-flagged floor of the chancel of the great 'Wool' church, rebuilt by him, as the brass proclaims, in the year 1401. Some portions of this splendid church date back to Norman times; others from Grevel's own century, while other and later portions have been skilfully incorporated.

Other buildings that are outstanding in a township in which it is hard to find a false note struck include the early-seventeenth-century William Hicks Almshouses, fronting on to a raised stone terrace on the main street (upper picture); the Town Hall; and Woolstaplers Hall, a stone building with a roof that is magnificent even by Cotswold standards. It was built in 1340 – the year of Chaucer's birth – by a family of traders in wool, the staple industry of the district, a family named Calf, who are commemorated, after six centuries, in Calf's Lane, which passes behind the Hall. From here, the 'staples' of wool would be carried by trains of pack ponies to the Channel ports.

It is now, however, a museum and, for its size, quite one of the most interesting small museums in the country. You will find penny-farthing bicycles, butter-churns and other pieces of domestic and agricultural equipment; a display of old lamps; a collection of silver cups and bowls, a mid-seventeenth-century box-mangle operated by stone weights, and much else besides. For all that, what makes the strongest, most lasting, impression is the town itself: venerable stone buildings from the fourteenth-century onwards, notable for their mullioned windows, stone-slab roofs, oriels and dormers, gables and ornamental dripstones, wholly satisfying to the eye and spirit alike.

30

Gloucestershire

CIRENCESTER

Colchester, Winchester, Leicester, Lancaster – wherever the Romans moved in, even if for only a short time, they left their mark; here too. For a long time this was the second largest town in Roman-occupied Britain, their Corinium. What remains of their presence is not immediately obvious; but the Corinium Museum is justly famous, one of the most important of its kind in the country.

There was an abbey here in the twelfth century, when the town had long been a Saxon stronghold after the Romans' departure; destroyed at the Dissolution, it left as its sole relic the Spital Gate, which had been at the north end of the abbey precincts. Wool brought enormous wealth to the town, as to other Cotswold towns such as Northleach; in the sixteenth century it possessed 'the greatest market of wool in all England'. The magnificent fifteenth-century Parish Church of St John the Baptist, with its glorious tower, is among the most beautiful not merely in the county but in the whole country. Among its most impressive features is the superb three-storeyed, fan-vaulted porch (opposite), designed in the Perpendicular style. It not only faces the Market Place but may be said to be an integral part of the traditional market, for it juts out across the pavement right into the midst of shoppers and passers-by; it is the best example in England of the age-old link between the sacred and the secular, seen more often in France than here. It was built later than the main body of the church, dating from 1500, and the two upper storeys were deliberately designed to serve for business rather than merely as an impressive ornamental entrance. From the seventeenth century onwards the upper chambers contained within the elaborately carved stonework, at once massive and graceful, served as Town Hall and Municipal Offices.

The great glory of the buildings here is the pale golden Cotswold stone. It is to be seen on every hand: in Park Street and Cecily Hall, in the famous Weavers' Hall in Thomas Street, beneath the gables of Dollar Street, on both sides of Coxwell Street and the great castellated wall of Cirencester Park. There is no market hall, as such; but the cattle market is still held here on the Tetbury Road, and on the first Monday in September the even more famous Sheep Fair is held annually; a reminder of Cirencester's importance as a sheep and wool centre from the Middle Ages onwards. 'Queen of the Cotswolds', the town likes to be called: difficult to dispute the title!

DORCHESTER

As with Chichester and Cirencester, the name of this town reveals its origin: when the Romans had ousted the Iron Age tribes from near-by Maiden Castle, they established themselves here and named the place Durnovaria. Portions of the encircling wall are still to be seen, notably in one of the avenues known today as The Walks, and relics of Neolithic, Iron Age and Roman occupation are to be seen in the very fine Dorset County Museum. Thomas Hardy, who renamed it 'Casterbridge' (retaining the Roman association), was born, lived and died within a very short distance of the town; of it he wrote: 'It announced old Rome in every street, alley and precinct. It looked Roman, bespoke the art of Rome, and concealed the dead men of Rome.'

It remained important from the Romans' time onwards. King Alfred's grandson, Athelstan, established a mint here; King John stayed in the Norman castle (of which little remains today); the infamous Judge Jeffreys held his 'Bloody Assizes' here in 1685, when he sentenced 292 prisoners to death. His lodgings were in High West Street (upper picture); his Court Room was at the rear of the *Antelope Hotel;* his chair and table may be seen today in the Council Chamber. A century and a half later, the 'Tolpuddle Martyrs' were sentenced to transportation, here in Dorchester, for the crime of seeking an increase in their weekly wage from nine shillings to ten.

Most of the houses are built of the cold grey stone of the district; relatively few are old, for a town with so ancient a tradition. For in 1613 Dorchester was swept by a fire that broke out in a tallow chandler's premises (as it was to do in 1731 in neighbouring Blandford Forum) and three hundred dwellings were destroyed. Nevertheless the long, climbing High Street presents an attractive and unified throughway, and among its outstanding buildings is the Shire Hall, where the Tolpuddle men learned their appalling fate.

Thomas Hardy, of course, dominates his 'Casterbridge'. An architect before he became a novelist, he designed Max Gate, his home on the edge of the town; at the top of High West Street is the Hardy Memorial, something of a shrine to lovers of the Wessex novels; and in the County Museum there is a recreation of the study (lower picture) in which they were written; here is his desk, his wallet and writing materials, his paperknife and magnifying glass, his letter-balance, ink-well, blotting pad and – most intimately – his delicately fashioned pince-nez.

Somerset

DUNSTER

You might protest that this is more village than market town (indeed I have written of it elsewhere as a village); but it is included here because of its quite outstanding Market Hall, at the upper end of its single wide, steeply sloping street. Known alternatively as the Yarn Market and the Butter Cross (upper picture), it dominates the place, catching the visitor's eye even before the huge mass of Dunster Castle rising from its tree-clad bluff at the southern end of the street. The two names bespeak the purposes the building has served: a meeting-place for trade, whether of wool or yarn or of good Somerset butter and other dairy products. It gives the township status: an eight-sided plinth of russet-coloured, well-worn stone carries a wide, thick, oaken sill which in turn forms the base for the squat, massive pillars that support a low-slung, two-pitched tiled roof inset with bold gables each containing a mullioned, lead-paned window; above all is a gabled lantern, the apex of the solid stone pillar about which the whole structure, dating from 1589, as it were revolves.

Opposite the Yarn Market stands the *Luttrell Arms,* now a hotel though it was built some five centuries ago as a 'town residence for the Abbot of Cleeve'. It is a lovely building in its own right, nobly proportioned, of beautifully quarried stone, its doorways and windows in particular catching the eye, especially the medieval porch. But then there is hardly a building, large or small, on either side of this street that does not arrest the attention: white façades, brickwork, half-timbering, stone, slate-hung walls, tiles and thatch abound. One of the slate-hung buildings was originally the guest house for the vanished twelfth-century priory.

Older by a good deal, however, is the other outstanding main feature, Dunster Castle (lower picture). It was founded over nine centuries ago, in 1070, and has been in continuous occupation ever since, and is so to this day. William de Bohun built it on its commanding site immediately after the Norman Conquest; in the fourteenth century it passed into the hands of the Luttrell family. It is they who no doubt imparted to this little market town the feudal atmosphere of which you swiftly become conscious as you wander about it even today. Explore the few narrow side streets at the foot of the main street: they are strongly medieval in 'feel', and you will come to what was once a nunnery, and also the old Castle Mill.

EVESHAM

Few would deny that this is the most beautiful town in the fruit-growing Vale to which it has given its name. Near enough to the Cotswolds to possess many examples of limestone buildings, and to the former great forests of Warwickshire to have also many notable examples of half-timbering, it thus has the best of both worlds. Like Malmesbury, it had its origin in a community that evolved round a Benedictine abbey, though this is largely ruined, having been used as a quarry, no less! Evesham is unique in that it has two parish churches, those of All Saints and of St Lawrence. Happily, the glorious 110ft bell-tower, completed by the last abbot in 1539, survives on the site of the former abbey; it is, again uniquely, shared by the two churches. On its peal of twelve bells, in addition to the quarter-hours, no fewer than fourteen tunes are played, in a series of recitals every three hours of the day.

The Norman gateway to the abbey, which was actually founded in AD 714, is a glorious example of building in stone, though it is not complete; above it is a fine example of half-timbering in the form of a Tudor upstairs chamber. But half-timbering is to be seen at its best here in a curious fifteenth-century three-storey structure known as the Booth Hall. For some inexplicable reason it is known also as the 'Round House' (lower picture), though it has vertical timbers, is straight sided and carries huge overhanging, sharp-pointed gables. It dominates the scene, as do so many of these market halls, houses and crosses in towns that flourished in medieval times.

Another splendid example of building, this time demonstrating the skilful blending of stonework and half-timbering, is the Almonry (upper picture) on Merstow Green. During the centuries when the abbey flourished, this was where the Almoner distributed alms to the needy of the district. It stands close to two medieval buildings that incorporated the original abbey gateway; it now serves, appropriately, as a museum, the exhibits in which portray the life and industry of the locality from medieval times onwards. In front of the Almonry is a set of stocks protected by a roof of Cotswold slate similar to that of the Almonry itself. Beautiful as the individual buildings are, however, it is probably true to say that the most memorable element in Evesham is its air of serenity: a loop of the quiet River Avon, greensward, trees, a sense of permanence and of contentment that is all-pervading.

FARNHAM

Lying amid pleasant country, on the border of Surrey and Hampshire, in spite of its relative proximity to London and to the network of trunk roads all about it, the town has contrived to preserve much of its old-world charm. Though its chiefly memorable features are its elegant Georgian houses, its display of red and russet brickwork, its origins and the reason for its substantial appearance date from many centuries earlier. Its castle dates from the latter part of the twelfth century, when it was built to the orders of that great castle-building monarch, Henry II, to replace an earlier one. It possesses, incidentally, not merely one of the finest examples of a Norman Shell Keep but, in its Great Chapel, some outstanding examples of fourteenth- to seventeenth-century carvings. You may wonder why such a chapel survives to this day; the reason is that this has been the seat of the Bishops of Winchester and Guildford, much occupied by them, and indeed by the latter bishop until as recently as 1956. Monarchs from Edward I to Victoria have been entertained within its walls.

Farnham was granted its Charter by the Bishop of Winchester in 1248 and retained Corporate status until 1789; it was a wool market of great importance; in the seventeenth century it was, as that great traveller Defoe reported, 'the greatest corn market in England, London excepted'; later it became a hop-growing centre; all in all, it has been, and remains, a thriving market town with a long and honoured tradition.

If the castle is impressive, it is perhaps the individual streets and the houses in them that leave the more intimate impression. Castle Street, for instance, which is lined with some of the most outstanding Georgian buildings to be found in any small country town and in which the Old Almshouses (upper picture) are to be seen. Another fine street is West Street, where a particularly notable example of architecture is to be found: Wilmer House, dating from the early eighteenth century, now contains the local museum. Just off West Street is a quiet and picturesque backwater, the Lion and Lamb Courtyard (lower picture). You should wander at your leisure in these streets and small courtyards leading off them, to find something memorable whichever way you turn. Incidentally, Farnham is the birthplace of William Cobbett, author of *Rural Rides*; he was buried in the graveyard of the parish church, which happens to possess one of the comparatively rare 'Vinegar' Bibles.

FROME

In the Domesday Book this market town ranked with Bath – the only other one in the county with borough status. Its focal point is its Market Place near the bridge over the river which shares its name. Off this runs the sloping Cheap (or Market) Street, parts of it paved with (a reminder of medieval conditions even in London) a central watercourse, formerly a drain but now just a lively little channel. On either side are gabled houses, many of them half-timbered, but the street is essentially a pedestrian precinct, narrow enough to be spanned with wrought-iron arches bearing lamps or, as with a baker's shop, its trademark: an old-fashioned (long regretted!) 'cottage loaf'.

There is no market hall as such, but the town lies on the fringe of the sheep-grazing country and so became involved in the wool and cloth industry. Evidence of its prosperity is seen on every hand, even in the quality of its smaller houses of good local stone and craftsmanship, as shown in the row overlooking the stream that runs alongside Willow Vale (lower picture). They would not be out of place in any Cotswold township, though the limestone here is notably paler than that to the north.

Other buildings of note include the Parish Church of St John the Baptist, built over the years between the twelfth and fifteenth centuries but containing some Norman and even some Saxon remains; it is to be found at the top of Cheap Street. Purists may deplore the 'Victorianisation' of parts of the interior, as did Frome folk; happily the outspoken Bishop Ken, who lies buried in the churchyard, had died two centuries earlier! More unusual, however, is the curious 'Blue House' in the Market Place. It was erected long, long ago as 'a sanctuary and Home for Elderly Frome Ladies'. It was restored not long ago, and in a niche above the entrance, beneath the high roof with its cupola and clock, stands an effigy in stone of one of the elderly ladies of Frome for whom it was designed.

Much of this market town is now being developed and extended in all directions, as is so often the case. But its centre still contains the 'olde-worlde' element beloved of the visitor. One representative example of this is King Street (upper picture), seen looking downwards from the top. Like many of Frome's streets it is on a substantial slope, and the buildings on either side of it give the impression of 'elbowing' their way up it – or, on the other hand, of bracing themselves against one another to avoid slipping down the hill!

HELMSLEY

One's instinct is often to be wary of North Yorkshire towns, on the quite unreasonable assumption that they must be grey, gaunt, harsh, unwelcoming, wholly lacking in the picturesque. This old market town, Elmeslac in Domesday (which gives proof of its antiquity), certainly disproves this assumption. It has an immediately welcoming air, whether you approach it from the north-west by way of Rievaulx Abbey or across the bridge spanning the River Wye to the south. Its vast Market Place, startlingly spacious for so relatively small, even 'cosy', a town, seems to hold out its arms to you; its display of houses large and small, old and not-so-old, which frame it on all four sides, seem to open their doors and windows to you. In the very heart of the Market Place, which is on a decided slope, stands the ancient Market Cross on its square plinth of sixth well-worn steps. The houses range from grey, weathered stone to half-timbering – not found all that often in North Yorkshire.

The building that dominates the Market Place is the *Black Swan* (opposite), which looms over it from its upper edge. The building incorporates two Georgian houses, some half-timbering, and what was at one time the rectory for the Parish Church of All Saints. This itself appears less old than you might anticipate, for it was much restored just over a century ago; but it contains some relics of its Norman origin, notably the South Porch. At the opposite end of the time-scale it contains a set of interesting murals recording the story of Christianity down the ages, planned a hundred years ago and completed in 1909.

On the outskirts of the town is what remains of the castle, the earliest portions of which date back to the year 1200. It is noteworthy for its remarkable series of immense double fortification-ditches, its barbican and its West Tower; and also (for the castle was the home down the centuries of a succession of distinguished families such as the Rutlands and the Dukes of Buckingham) for some fine Tudor interiors, windows and panelling. In addition to the castle, now preserved by the Department of the Environment, and the church, there are unexpected treasures to be found; for example, the half-timbered Tudor building known as Canons' Garth, named after the canons of Kirkham Priory, though subsequently it was to know humbler occupants, having served intermittently as a modest vicarage, a pair of cottages, and as a doss-house for vagrants.

HEXHAM

The greatest glory of this town, set on the south bank of the river just below the confluence of the North and South Tyne, is the Priory Church of St Andrew (upper picture), begun by the Augustinians in the very early twelfth century and incorporating much earlier work. There was a Saxon church here in the eighth century, and you may enter the crypt (lower right), which was constructed by the Saxons with stones taken from the Corstopitum (Corbridge) section of Hadrian's Wall, built during the Roman occupation centuries earlier. Another link between the legionaries and the Saxons to be seen here is the strikingly realistic monument to Flavinus in which a standard-bearer is riding-down a fallen Saxon who holds an upraised dagger in his hand (lower left). In the Choir you may see the famous Frith Stool (originally St Wilfrid's Chair): it was used for Northumbrian coronation ceremonies; it was also a guarantee of sanctuary for any felon or refugee who could ensconce himself in it.

Though it may be thought of as a minor cathedral city, Hexham has in fact always been a market centre, one of the most important in the North Country. Its focal point is the Market Place, overlooked by the priory church. Within a stone's-throw or less of this are other noteworthy buildings. The forbidding twelfth-century grey stone Moot Hall, for instance, originally the gateway to Hexham Castle, for centuries housed the so-called Court of Regalities; there is a hint of its original portcullis in its stonework. Here too is The Shambles, the old name for the slaughter-house; of later date, it was used by vendors in the poultry and butter market. Close by is a vastly older building, the oddly named Manor Office. This dates from 1330, when it was built to serve as a gaol – the first building to be specifically designed for this purpose. The Steward of the Regality was instructed to install manacles and chains, and a local barber, one John de Cawode, was appointed official gaoler at a wage of two pence per day. The stone of which its nine-foot-thick walls were constructed came from the remains of a Roman building on the north bank of the Tyne.

Street names evoke ancient and medieval times, often with a hint of 'story' in them: Battle Hill; Hencotes; St Wilfrid's Gate; Tanners Row; Giles Gate; Priestpopple – the 'Street of the Priests' People', part of the main road leading to the cattle market. Here, on a beautiful riverside site, the ancient, the very old, the medieval and the relatively new are all unobtrusively integrated.

46

Buckinghamshire

HIGH WYCOMBE

Until as recently as 1946 this town was known also as Chepping (Chipping) Wycombe – evidence, as in the case of towns like Chipping Campden and Chipping Sodbury, that it was an established centre for sale and exchange of local and other products; it had served in this capacity for more than three centuries. Now that it has been by-passed by the M40 Motorway (from which an excellent near-aerial panoramic view may be obtained) there is a fair chance that the essence of this Chiltern town will remain unspoiled. Certainly there is no risk that its fine Guildhall (upper picture), built by Henry Keene in 1757 to replace a timber structure erected in 1604, will be damaged by traffic. Of mellow brick with stone dressings and topped by a lantern tower with a weather-vane depicting a centaur shooting an arrow into the wind, it dominates the junction of High Street and Paul's Row. The arcades of stone columns support a well-windowed upper storey containing the Council Chamber; on market days the stalls are set out behind them. Wool, woollen products, plaited straw and lace were among the town's earlier products; now it is mainly chair-making, of Chiltern beech.

Opposite the Guildhall, scheduled as an Ancient Monument, is another and smaller building, the Little Market House, or Shambles. Octagonal in shape, with two wings and arcaded, it was designed by the famous Robert Adam in 1761, its low domed roof and cupola, however, being later additions. Of the two, this is certainly the more picturesque. Look carefully behind the arcade and you will discover a panel setting out the tolls demanded of the stall holders, reminiscent of those to be seen on our few surviving toll-bridges, as at Hay-on-Wye for example.

In the Parish Church of St Nicholas, the town possesses the largest church in the county. Its essentially Norman origin is to be seen in the South Porch, though the interior is mainly fourteenth and fifteenth century work, notably the south chancel screen erected by Richard Redehole in 1468. The tower, dominating the roof tops, contains a fine peal of twelve bells, worthy of the church and its setting and tradition. Move away from the centre and you will come upon the most charming backwaters (lower picture). Some of them have water as the dominant feature; others a fine stand or two of trees, notably beeches for which the region is famous; or an elegant private house with sweeping lawn and terrace.

HITCHIN

This old market town is of outstanding interest because though it is relatively near to London it is so little spoiled, retaining much of its medieval layout. It bestrides the River Hiz (once the name of the town) and is girt about by smaller rivers: Oughton, Purwell and Ippollitts Brook. Its focal point is the great Market Place. From its four corners radiate four streets all with buildings of note, including *Red Hart Inn* (lower picture) in Bucklersbury. High Street has some admirable eighteenth-century buildings and leads into Bancroft (upper picture), which has Georgian and Regency buildings but, most notably, a superb example of medieval half-timbering. The beautiful fourteenth-century gate-house, with overhanging gable, diamond-paned windows and oak timbers, is in fact the entrance to a manufacturing chemist. This typifies the town's determination to maintain traditional style where possible without impeding industrial progress. Just beyond are the Skynner Almshouses, dating from 1670.

Sun Street leads to Bridge Street, with its many timber-framed buildings with overhanging storeys; this continues as Tilehouse Street, with medieval, half-timbered buildings and, again, Regency and Georgian. There is, too, a relatively modern Baptist Church, built on the site of the one in which John Bunyan preached; it has his own chair as part of its pulpit. Unlike many market towns of comparable age, Hitchin does not have a medieval Market Hall, though there is in fact a particularly fine fifteenth-century half-timbered building in the Market Place. It does, however, possess a Victorian Corn Exchange in Italianate style with, to emphasise this, a Venetian window, and also a remarkable lantern turret.

Among the town's many historic inns is *The Sun*, in Sun Street, whence the first Hitchin coach departed on its lengthy journeys in 1706. On record here is a Manorial Dinner which included a whole sheep, a quarter of beef and three pigs – for 26 shillings in all! Opposite the Market Square is the Parish Church of St Mary the Virgin, built in the fifteenth century (with some evidence of much earlier work) in a style commensurate with the affluence of the wool traders who flourished here, as in Suffolk. Its embattled exterior, with turreted tower, is extremely impressive. Inside, it contains some of the finest woodwork in the county, in its screen and particularly in its bench-ends, among other examples of master-craftsmen's skills.

HORSHAM

This town makes no claim to Roman origin, but it certainly flourished in early medieval times and onwards, for it was a centre (hard to credit today!) for the smelting of Wealden iron from the local iron ore, as a result of which the vast surrounding forests were depleted. In 1461 it was granted the right to hold two fairs annually as well as its long established markets. One of these coincided with the Assizes, first held here in 1306; because of the number of executions carried out at the then County Gaol it came to be known as 'Hang Fair'. Until as recently as 1850 the sign 'WIVES FOR SALE' could be seen here on these occasions in Market Square.

As at Chichester, four compass-point roads radiate from the centre, known as Carfax – *'carre-four'*; Oxford is the only other English town to possess a Carfax. Close by is the seventeenth-century Town Hall, the barred lower windows of which remind the visitor that the old Town Gaol was beneath the main chamber; here, until last century, felons were condemned to execution or transportation to Botany Bay. Look out also for a box inset in the stonework and inscribed 'Ye Olde Post Box of Horsham'.

There are sixteenth-century buildings in Pump Alley (the name bespeaks its origin); thence runs The Causeway, a cul-de-sac with many interesting buildings, some dating from Tudor times. There is the historic Hewells Manor House, for instance; and The Chantry, the Old Priest's House; and, perhaps most interesting of all, Causeway House, a mid-sixteenth-century merchant's dwelling (like that in Fore Street, Totnes, Devon) which now houses the local museum. Here are exhibits of domestic and agricultural interest, including bicycles and horse-brasses, ploughs and other farm implements, a reconstituted saddler's shop and wheelwright's shop and an old-time Sussex kitchen. Behind, old farm buildings are being re-assembled to house other features such as Sussex wagons. It is here that you will see at their best roofs formed from the celebrated Horsham slabstone. This is to be found in many streets; it is also to be found, more substantially, as pavements (both pictures).

The whole scene is dominated by the Parish Church of St Mary, parts of which date back to the twelfth century – notably the 800-year-old massive yellow sandstone tower capped by a slender wooden-shingled spire; in Horsham the medieval and the truly old and the modern are in nice juxtaposition.

KENDAL

The slightly enigmatic motto of this important market town, *Pannus Mihi Panis*, is interesting. Though the Romans established bases near by, associated with Hadrian's Wall just to the north; and though the Saxons occupied the present site (a cross-shaft dating from AD 850 may be seen in the south aisle of the church), Kendal really came into prominence in 1189 when Richard Coeur-de-Lion made it a barony; in 1331 Edward III granted it a Weavers' Charter, and from then onwards the town flourished as the chief centre of wool weaving in the North. 'Kendal Green' (a tough cloth worn by English archers) was made here, and the industry throve for six hundred years: 'Wool, indeed, was the town's Bread.' In the intervening years, however, it had been repeatedly ravished by the Scottish Borderers, and it is believed that the steep, narrow alleys known as 'yards', or 'courts', such as Dr Manning's Yard (upper picture), were designed to afford refuge for Kendal folk and barriers to the invaders; also, they led to the cottages where the Flemish weavers worked.

Happily, this lovely country town, the 'Auld Grey Toon', has now been by-passed by a motorway and thus should preserve its sense of history for all time. It is indeed redolent of history. In the now dilapidated Norman Castle, Catherine Parr, the only one of Henry VIII's six wives to survive him, was born; the thirteenth-century Parish Church of the Holy Trinity, one of the largest in England, has five aisles: into this church Robin Philipson, Royalist, rode his charger to seek revenge on Colonel Briggs, Roundhead, while at prayer, as described by Scott in *Rokeby*. In the present YWCA building Bonnie Prince Charlie, on his way north after his defeat at Derby, slept one night; two nights later, the murderous Duke of Cumberland, in pursuit, occupied the same bed!

In front of the relatively new Town Hall are the remains of the old Market Cross; it is known as the Call Stone, for from time immemorial monarchs of England have been proclaimed there. From the high Town Hall tower, six times a day, a carillon plays a succession of English, Welsh, Scottish and Irish tunes, each country's tunes having a day to itself. Old and not-so-old objects are on display in the fascinating Museum of Lakeland Life and Industry, and also in the Borough Museum; and an unusual 'museum' exists in the Castle Dairy (lower picture), built in the year of Shakespeare's birth, 1564, and showing in detail many features of Tudor domestic architecture.

KESWICK

Standing as it does midway between Penrith and St Bees Head, to east and west, and Furness Abbey and Gretna Green to south and north, it is at the true heart of English Lakeland. The northern tip of Derwentwater (for many Lake lovers the most beautiful) reaches so close to the town's heart that it is often called 'Keswick-on-Derwentwater'; the southern tip of Bassenthwaite approaches close to its outskirts from the north; the 3,000ft mass of Skiddaw towers above the grey slate roofs and the walls of slate or white-painted roughcast picked out with black window-frames.

Most visitors use it merely as a springboard for exploration of the valleys and fells, mountain passes and screes; or they come to tread the ways known to the 'Lakeland School' of poets, Scott and Lamb, Ruskin (who observed that Keswick was 'a place too beautiful to live in'), to Robert Louis Stevenson, and to Hugh Walpole of the *Herries Chronicles* whose home was hard by, overlooking the lake. But Keswick has plenty of interest in its own right. Narrow lanes lead into and out of it, its unusual Market Place being really no more than a temporary widening of its main road.

Here you will find its unusual Market House, or Moot Hall (opposite). It cannot vie in age with those of countless others up and down the country, for it was built only in 1813, replacing an earlier one. Its alternative name indicates that, as so often, the town's business and justice was carried on within. It is endearingly small: a sort of campanile with a high-arched entrance at ground level, a semi-circular window, a clock – which has, by design, only one hand – and another and larger window and a graceful little roof. The whole gives the appearance of having been 'tacked on' to the main building behind it, up the slope and standing clear of the shops on either side; it might have been transplanted from, say, the Ticino and come happily to rest here and see out its days amid scenery that can well be compared with that of Switzerland, if on a minor scale. All about it, branching off the straight main street, are alluring little alleyways, leading who knows whither – until you have explored them for yourself. No buildings of any great architectural distinction, it must be admitted; but this is a close-knit, homely little market town, known (as its name implies) to the Scandinavians who sailed up the Furness and other estuaries a thousand years ago or thereabouts, and settled in the district.

KING'S LYNN

This market-seaport appears in Domesday as Lun; in the twelfth century it was Bishop's Lynn; in 1204 King John granted it a Royal Charter and it has been King's Lynn ever since. It was built on three reclaimed marshy islands washed by four streams flowing into the Ouse, and early became England's third most thriving port, with two markets and two guildhalls. The famous Saturday Market was established in the early twelfth century, the equally famous Tuesday Market fifty years later; they are held to this day, at opposite ends of the enormous Market Place. Each market has its own church: those of St Margaret and St Nicholas. In medieval times this was a walled town; even today you enter by the imposing South Gate (lower picture), the one survivor; it leads straight to the Market Place.

There is hardly a street or corner that does not possess more than one building of historic interest, fine buildings ranging from the twelfth to the nineteenth century. Trinity Guildhall dates from 1421: like the much later Town Hall, it is an impressive example of flint 'chequer-board' work. Inside is the town's regalia, including the King John gilded cup, and his sword. Not far away is the so-called *Greenland Fishery Inn*, base of the whaler-men who brought much prosperity from Greenland waters; St Margaret's Church was for centuries, until 1829, lit by whale-oil lamps. Across the way from Hampton Court, which was first built in 1200, though it is largely fourteenth-century, you will find The Steelyard – a warehouse belonging to the Hanseatic League whose most famous warehouses are in Bergen, Norway; built of brick and timber, it skirts St Margaret's Lane. In St James's Street, Greyfriars (one of many monastic foundations) dates from the thirteenth century. Later, even more interesting, is Red Mount Chapel. It stands on a slight rise, is octagonal in shape and was used as a resting-place for pilgrims bound for the shrine of Our Lady of Walsingham, some miles to the east.

Later still is the famous Customs House (upper picture), erected in 1683: a classical-style two-storey edifice with dormer windows in a roof topped by a balustrade reminiscent of the Market Hall at Abingdon. It carries an elegant lantern tower, with a stone niche containing a statue of Charles II to whom, alone among East Anglian boroughs, King's Lynn remained loyal. But this bare catalogue does not begin to do justice to this unusual market-town-cum-seaport; it must be seen and wandered in to be experienced.

North Yorkshire

KNARESBOROUGH

It is no exaggeration to state that this is one of the most picturesque, and spectacularly sited, of all our market towns. Like North Yorkshire's Richmond, which dominates the steep gorge of the Swale, this old town dominates that of the River Nidd. The most impressive view of it (upper picture) is from the grounds of the castle, first built on this rocky bluff three years after the Norman Conquest, though what remains today is largely fourteenth-century. See especially John O'Gaunt's Keep.

The little town is exceptionally rich in historic records. In the museum in the keep you may see, for instance, suits of armour worn at the Battle of Marston Moor and other relics. Near the entrance to the castle there is the medieval Court of Knaresborough, a fourteenth-century building on which, three centuries later, an upper storey was superimposed. Here, the three men who actually murdered Thomas à Becket hid for three anxious years. Here Richard II was imprisoned while on his way to his death at Pontefract. On the far side of Low Bridge is the recess in the sandstone cliff which served as dwelling for Mother Shipton, the strange figure whose many 'prophecies' included references to cars and aircraft, though she was uttering them more than four hundred years ago. Not far away is the famous Dropping Well (lower picture), the most remarkable example of a petrifying-well in the country; you will see suspended beneath the overhanging rock a grotesque array of small objects such as gloves, shoes, ornaments, toys and knots of rope, all now slowly but inexorably, and literally, being turned into stone by the action of the minerals in the water. Alchemy, or chemistry? Call it what you will; but in the Market Place you will find what is truly claimed to be 'Ye Oldest Chymist Shoppe in England'.

The town possesses, in the Castle Mill, the oldest linen mill in England, dating back to 1785 and operating until quite recently. John Metcalf – 'Blind Jack of Knaresborough' – was born here, predecessor of Telford and Macadam as bridge and road builder, a unique personality. Here too was born Eugene Aram, schoolmaster and murderer, whose victim's skeleton was unearthed two centuries ago in a cleft in the rock, long known as St Robert the Hermit's Cave. Thomas Hood told his story in ballad-like verses which many schoolchildren must know. All in all (for there is much else besides), this little town possesses more strange stories than most of its size.

Cornwall

LAUNCESTON

With the spectacular ruins of its Norman castle dominating it from the summit of a conical hill, best seen from the air (opposite), it is not difficult to accept the term 'feudal' to describe it, as well as its claim to be the 'Gateway to Cornwall'. Until 1838 it was in fact the county's capital; because of its commanding position it had been successively a Celtic settlement, a Saxon settlement and eventually a Norman stronghold; it may truly be said to breathe antiquity. Lying between two hills, the heart of the town has always been the setting for the famed agricultural market: established in the early eleventh century, it is held always on a Tuesday.

This is, of course, granite country. Apart from the magnificent ruins of the castle, the most outstanding example of the use of the stone here is unquestionably the triple-aisled Parish Church of St Mary Magdalene. This is in fact unique in all England, for, with the exception of its fourteenth-century tower, its granite walls are covered externally with ornate carving. In addition to the conventional designs there are the arms of the Kelway and Trecarrell families on the South Porch – it was Sir Henry Trecarrell who built the present church early in the fifteenth century; the arms of the then reigning monarch, Henry VIII, may be seen at the east end of the church; shields around the church bear such inscriptions as 'Hail Mary, Full of Grace' and 'This is No Other than the House of God and Gate of Heaven'.

Launceston was once a walled town. The South Gate survives intact, the two rooms above the archway having formerly served as a prison; later they housed the local museum, though this is now at Lawrence House, just below the castle. It is approached by way of Castle Street, where you will find that not all this feudal town is cold granite: there are many fine Georgian houses, of red brick with large windows and white-painted porticoes – as satisfying a contrast with the granite as can be imagined. The street is arrived at by way of Castle Green, where the last public hanging took place, in 1821. Beyond this is the so-called Doomsgate Tower in which George Fox, Founder of the Society of Friends, was incarcerated in 1656 for 'subversive activities'. Facing Castle Green is the Town Hall, Tudor in appearance but in fact not a hundred years old; it possesses an antique clock whose bell is struck every quarter-hour by two 'clock-jacks': thus, the ancient and the modern in juxtaposition.

LEDBURY

It would be difficult even in this area, which possesses many of the finest examples of half-timbering in all England, to find more than may be seen in this small, unassuming but most rewarding market town; many connoisseurs would select this as the most picturesque of its kind for a hundred miles in all directions. At the crossroads at its heart are three of the most memorable of its buildings. *Ye Olde Talbot,* built in 1596, has hardly changed in appearance outside or in since the day the last joiner downed his tools; it has some magnificent carved panelling and an impressive overmantel in its dining-room. *The Feathers,* with its many gables, is from the same period and is comparable with its opposite number at Ludlow, to the north.

Most impressive of all, and indeed one of the most remarkable of its kind in the whole country, is the great timber-framed Market House (lower picture), the work of the King's Carpenter, John Abel, who built it in 1617. It stands on the edge of the irregular Market Place, its herringbone-timbered upper storey supported on no fewer than sixteen pillars of Spanish chestnut. This is the focal point of Ledbury. At one time corn was stored beneath the roof, hoisted there in sacks through a trapdoor in the upper floor of the Great Hall, which was for centuries the Town Hall and administrative centre and court. On these pillars the town's edicts were posted; until less than a century ago itinerant companies of actors came here in horse-drawn wagons, complete with their 'props', for one-night fit-up performances.

The Market Place is linked with the twelfth-century Parish Church, which contains some Saxon work but is even more noteworthy for the unusual free-standing thirteenth-century stone tower whose steeple rises to over two hundred feet, by narrow Church Lane (upper picture). Its cobbles are overlooked by projecting timber upper storeys that almost meet overhead. Until 1746, horse-drawn gigs and traps could use it; then posts were installed to make this impossible. Perhaps nowhere else is one so conscious of the medieval 'feel' of the little town. It has literary associations, too, spanning the centuries. The poet Thomas Traherne was born here in 1636; three centuries earlier, William Langland, author of *Piers Plowman,* was born here; and in 1878 John Masefield, sometime Poet Laureate, was born here, and Ledbury and district formed the background and setting for three of his best-known narrative poems.

Staffordshire

LICHFIELD

Strictly speaking, this is a small cathedral city rather than a market town. It was the seat of the Bishopric of West Mercia in the seventh century; the cathedral, dedicated to St Chad, of mellow russet sandstone, was begun in the twelfth century and is the only one in England to have three steeples; they are picturesquely known as 'The Ladies of the Vale'. Near the cathedral is what remains of the medieval Minster Pool, one of a group that were an essential factor in the town's economy, which was based on dyeing and fulling cloth, on tanning and parchment-making and on milling corn. So it is fitting to consider this as a market town, and its cobbled Market Square is its true centre. It was here, incidentally, that Edward Wightman, the last man to be burned at the stake, died in agony in 1612; forty years later, George Fox, the Quaker, stood up in the Market Square after a hideous vision he had had of the town's streets running with martyr's blood, and cried: 'Woe to the bloody city of Lichfield!'

At the corner of Market Square stands the house (upper picture) in which Dr Samuel Johnson was born in 1709, appropriately enough the son of a bookseller who traded in these premises; his statue overlooks the Square, and is matched by a somewhat inferior statue of his biographer, James Boswell, a stone's throw away. Dr Johnson paid tribute to the town of his birth in the words 'Hail, Great Mother!'; suitably enough, Lichfield's official motto has become the Latinised *Salve, Magna Parens*.

It has developed over the years, and though you could hardly miss the roseate-hued cathedral with its triple spires, you may have to look carefully to find the Dame School (lower picture) attended by Johnson as a child. Dame Oliver is said to have reported of him even at that tender age: 'The best scholar I ever had.' You cannot miss the well-windowed, dignified building in which he was born, brilliantly white painted and flanked by tall columns. It is now a museum, and inside you will find personal mementoes that bring him to life (as in the Hardy Museum at Dorchester): his favourite armchair, his walking-stick, letters and manuscripts, and his silver teapot (he was a tremendous drinker of tea all his life). Not far away, in Dam Street, may be seen wood- and stone-carvers at work, carrying on an ancient tradition begun there when the Cathedral Church of St Chad was being built of the local red sandstone eight hundred years ago.

LUDLOW

Laid out in an almost perfect grid pattern in a crook formed by the River Teme and its tributary, the Corve, this is, with the exception perhaps of Bury St Edmunds, the earliest example of town-planning in the country, dating generally as it does from the twelfth century. It is dominated on its western side by the remains of Ludlow Castle, begun just after the Norman Conquest; for centuries, this was the official seat of the Lords-President of the Welsh Marches, and no other border town in this county or in neighbouring Hereford and Worcester surpasses it in interest and importance. Anglo-Saxon coins unearthed on the rising ground above the Teme prove that it was highly regarded for its strategic position even in those days; from Norman times onwards it was to serve as a bastion against the Welsh.

It naturally soon became a market town of importance. In the Middle Ages it was a collecting-point for the hill-country sheep whose wool was carried by pack-horse trains to Bristol for shipment abroad. Its Market Charter was granted in the fifteenth century and the market has been held on Mondays ever since. The focal point is the pseudo-classical Butter Cross, built in 1746 to replace a much older one; it stands at the top of the famous Broad Street (upper picture), which climbs from Ludford Bridge, almost every building in it dating from the fourteenth or fifteenth century; its upper room was once a Blue Coat Charity School but now houses a small and charming museum. Broad Gate (lower picture), through which this street has passed, is the sole survivor of the seven gates of the original town wall.

The town centre is scheduled as 'of special architectural interest'. Here is the Parish Church of St Laurence, substantially fifteenth-century; here too is the thirteenth-century timber-framed 'Reader's House'; and again, the late-Elizabethan *Feathers Hotel*, one of the noblest examples of half-timbering in all England. This stands in the triangular Bull Ring, where bulls were tethered on market days. There is also, as at Burford, a Tolsey. Here disputes were settled in what was known as Pied Powder Court since they had to be resolved 'while ye dust is still on ye feet'. Every other building, indeed, is of special interest, architecturally, historically, or otherwise. Devotees of *The Shropshire Lad* and *Last Poems* will want to see the grave of A. E. Housman, a modest, appropriate shrine. Ludlow can claim with justification to rank among our country towns richest in history as well as in beauty.

MALMESBURY

On the southern fringe of the Cotswolds and so in the 'limestone belt', this lovely old market town, incidentally one of the oldest boroughs in the land, is built largely of that incomparable stone. This is best seen in the triple-storeyed parish church, saved by a wealthy clothier who had set up his looms here after the dissolution of the Norman Benedictine abbey. In its South Porch is the tomb of Athelstan, grandson of King Alfred. Here you may see two finely sculptured panels depicting the Twelve Apostles (lower picture). From the long-since-vanished tower an eleventh-century monk named Elmer once projected himself in flight, allegedly covering a furlong before he landed and in doing so broke both legs.

An even more remarkable example of stonework is the sixteenth-century Market Cross (upper picture), regarded (with that at Chichester) as one of the two finest in the country. The historian Leland described it soon after it was erected as 'a right faire costley peace of work, curiously vaulted, for poore market folkes to stande dry when rayne cummith'. It rises to over forty feet at the tip of its beautifully carved pinnacle, is octagonal in form, with battlements, flying buttresses and statuettes of saints in symmetrically ordered niches.

There are also fragments of medieval buildings here and there, often incorporated in newer buildings. In the famous *Bell Hotel* near by may be found sections of walling that dates back to the thirteenth century, when the town was partly walled on its eminence above the Avon; in the same building there is a window that was once in the Guest House of the Abbot of Malmesbury. The seventeenth-century St John Almshouses stand on the site of a Saxon foundation and incorporate some Norman arches; they are of the same noble stone, and Athelstan contributed £10 annually towards their upkeep, a sum that is paid to this day! Abbey House was built by William Stumpe, the public-spirited clothier who saved the bulk of the abbey church at the Dissolution. It stands on the site of the original Abbot's House. Another hotel, the *White Lion*, may well have been part of the abbey buildings, which were very extensive and constantly added to from their foundation in Saxon times. In this quiet, withdrawn town you become aware not only of its medieval tradition but of its later development as a weaving town of importance with its heyday in the seventeenth and early eighteenth centuries; evidence of its affluence is all about you in the quality of its buildings.

Leicestershire

MARKET HARBOROUGH

Like Market Bosworth, in the same county, Market Drayton in Shropshire and Market Overton in Leicestershire, this name tells all, unmistakably. It has been established without question that there was a market held regularly here as far back as Norman times; in 1180 a Market Charter was granted to the town by Henry II. The importance of the town was largely due to the existence of a practicable ford across the River Welland which was in continuous use by traders and packhorse trains and was succeeded by a bridge as long ago as 1228. The town's wide main street rises gently from its unusual triangular Square which, as always with such towns, is its focal point. The outstanding feature here is the free-standing, half-timbered, elaborately gabled Market Hall (upper picture); this in itself is unique in that it was originally designed to serve as a grammar school, founded by Robert Smythe in 1614. The school occupied the main first-floor chamber; beneath this, the market itself was held, open of access by way of its great timber pillars and with a right-of-way from south to north. Here the farmers' wives of the district sold their dairy produce. There is also the famous Tuesday Sheep Market (lower picture).

On the opposite side of the High Street, beyond the Market Hall, is the most famous of the town's old inns, *The Three Swans*, a true coaching inn. Since the town is so near the centre of England, and on two important main roads, it formed a meeting place for coaches and wagons from north, south, east and west. The outstanding feature of this inn, today, is the superb eighteenth-century wrought iron sign hanging out over the pavement; Whyte-Melville immortalised the inn in his hunting novel (the town is famous for the Fernie Hunt), and the eccentric innkeeper, John Fothergill, gave it a new lease of life during the years prior to his death twenty years ago.

Almost facing the inn is the parish church, with its unusual dedication to St Dionysius. Its splendid crocketed broach spire dominates the rooftops of most of the town; the feature is not unique, indeed it is more usually seen in the south-east, but this fourteenth-century example is regarded by experts as one of the finest in all England. The church started life as nothing more than a chapel-of-ease, but has been enlarged and much restored. An odd tradition is maintained here: annually in November its bells are rung to commemorate the miraculous survival of a wealthy merchant 'lost amid the Welland Marshes'; the ringers receive one shilling each as 'beer money'.

MUCH WENLOCK

If the 'Much' in the town's name leads you to expect a large town, you will be pleasurably disillusioned! This is truly a small town, but its few short streets contain a wealth of ancient and picturesque buildings, even before you come to its best known, the seventh-century nunnery of St Milburga which was destroyed by the Danes in AD 874 and rebuilt as a priory of the Cluniac Order in Norman times. During the rebuilding, the remains of the saint were unearthed, to be enshrined on 26 May 1101, a day then established for the payment in future of all monastic dues. The priory (upper picture) is sadly dilapidated today, but the twelfth-century Chapter House is immensely impressive, and a curious feature is the twelfth-century *lavabo* with carvings of unusual distinction. The cloisters survive, and the towering wall of the South Transept and much of the Early English West Front. After the Dissolution, the East Block was converted into one of the finest examples of a monastic building turned secular.

In the little town itself the outstanding feature is the sixteenth-century Guildhall. Its end wall is of stonework dating from the thirteenth-century and was once the gaol; the main fabric consists of a medieval half-timbered chamber supported on massive oak posts; it leans outwards over the narrow street, its great gables facing those of Raynalds' Mansion opposite, which dates from 1682. One of the oak pillars served as a whipping-post and you can see the iron staples that held the malefactor's wrists while he suffered. To be seen here also is a set of stocks (lower picture), last used in 1852; they are on wheels, so that the victims could be paraded helpless around the town to be mocked, insulted, assaulted.

The open area behind the pillars constituted the butter market. The market was established in 1224, and in 1236 Henry III 'gave the town his Royal Protection'. The Great Chamber above has huge cross-timbers and tie-beams and Jacobean panelling. It was long used as the Court Room, and bears a curious Latin inscription which, deciphered and then translated, states that 'This Place Abhors Iniquity, Loves Peace, Punishes Wrongdoing, Upholds the Law'. There is also, unexpectedly, a United States Forces Memorial Tablet, which links the ancient with the modern. Other features of this quite entrancing little place include St Owen's Well-house, a rare example of cruck-construction; thirteenth-century Holy Trinity Church; and a number of small half-timbered houses of modest beauty.

NANTWICH

As in neighbouring Middlewich and Northwich, the 'wich' in the name indicates the existence of salt, a commodity so essential that during the Roman occupation of Britain part of the legionaries' wage was paid in the form of *salarium* – hence our word salary. This trio of salt-producing towns has been important for some two thousand years; two of them remain so today, but Nantwich alone has any claim to picturesqueness. It possesses over a hundred buildings, large and small, scheduled as meriting preservation for their historic or architectural distinction. Indirectly, this is the result of a disastrous fire which broke out here in 1583 and raged for three weeks; the town was rebuilt in Elizabethan and Tudor styles, and there are not many towns in the country of this size that can boast so many fine examples. One reason for the quality of materials and workmanship is that Elizabeth I took pity on Nantwich (where there had been no fewer than four hundred modest salt refineries at work) and contributed not only money but timber from the neighbouring Royal Forest of Delamere for their construction.

One noteworthy example on a small scale is the *Crown Inn*, with its famous and, for an inn, most unusual Long Gallery on its uppermost floor. Another is the half-timbered building in Welsh Row known today as the *Cheshire Cat* but originally Widows' Almshouses. Here six widows, in pairs, were accommodated by the gift of Roger Wilbraham. Even more notable, however, is the magnificent timbered building – the timbers so massive that there is more black in evidence than the white plaster-work and many are curved as well as vertical and horizontal.

This house, still called Churche's Mansion (both pictures), was originally built for a wealthy merchant, one Richard Churche, whose name it bears. In his day it had a moat (like the better-known Little Moreton Hall in the same county). Built in 1577, it miraculously escaped the fire which, six years later, destroyed nearly six hundred dwellings, during which time the stricken townsfolk were also terrorised by bears which had escaped from their captivity in the yard of the *Bear Inn*. Much of the interior of the house has been maintained as it was in the merchant's day; panelling has been revealed, and also a contemporary well that made his household self-sufficient. It had a second narrow escape in 1930, when it came near to being dismantled and shipped to America; happily two local worthies acted in the matter in time.

NEWBURY

This was a settlement in Anglo-Saxon times. Though nothing remains today, it was a strongpoint in Norman times. Thanks to the by-pass road, all that is best of the medieval and later features now seems likely to survive. Among these are the Jacobean Cloth Hall (upper picture), near the Market Place, a reminder that this was a centre of the cloth trade. Indeed, the town owes much to 'Jack o' Newbury', a wealthy cloth merchant named John Smallwood who had no fewer than two hundred looms working for him and lived sufficiently well to be able to entertain Henry VIII in his house. It exists still, in Northbrook Street, adjoining a hotel that bears his name. He began the building of the Church of St Nicholas, completed by his son in 1532. The Cloth Hall was built in the seventeenth century as a workshop to give employment to impoverished labourers and artisans; oak pillars support its overhang, and it is fitting that it should now house a museum of particular local interest.

At the foot of Broadway there is a neat octagonal, stone-pillared and stepped Market Cross carrying a turret with a clock and serving today mainly as a shelter. Though Northbrook Street – one of the most notable main streets in any market town – is the most interesting, it is in the side-streets and alleys that, as usual, many of the most picturesque small buildings are to be found; as in Kendal, in Cumbria, they are known as 'courts'. Many of the cottage walls are tile hung – as in Kent; there is brick-and-timber-and-plasterwork; there is a general air of intimacy, of life-behind-closed-shutters, that smacks of medievalism. The same element is found in the row of Weavers' Cottages, Jacobean in origin, with moulded barge-boards, timber framing, gabled and sometimes tile hung, overlooking the little River Kennet. There is a cluster of seventeenth-century buildings, a medieval farmhouse converted into almshouses and now dedicated to retired nurses. In strong contrast is the substantial nineteenth-century Corn Exchange (lower picture). Inevitably, however, you will return to Northbrook Street for the overall view, a notable feature of which is the way that Georgian and even late-Georgian buildings, many of them now converted into shops, contrive to look not out of place among buildings both older and much more modern. To see the street at its best, view it from the upper end, beyond the little bridge spanning the Kennet in whose quiet waters the buildings are reflected.

Leicestershire

OAKHAM

One of the two townships (the other being Uppingham) in what was our smallest county, Rutland, it possesses a disproportionately large number of interesting features. One of these is the medieval timbered Butter Cross (upper picture), with a heavy roof constructed of the famous Collyweston slates supported on eight oak pillars and, in addition, an octagonal centre pillar of stone on a two-tier plinth. Housed beneath it are the old stocks, showing signs of sustained use down the years, reminiscent of those at, for example, Feock in Cornwall and Colne in Lancashire, and elsewhere.

   Not far away is an even more interesting building. This is the Great Hall (lower picture) of the near-vanished twelfth-century fortified manor. Sixty feet in length and forty feet in width, massively columned, it is one of the finest surviving specimens of its kind in the country. Its most unusual feature (it is open to the public) is its astonishing collection of horseshoes. Formerly it was an Assize Court, and by statute every monarch, or member of the nobility, who had occasion to pass through Oakham had to present to the town a toll in the form of a horseshoe. The custom was instituted by William the Conqueror, whose Farrier-in-Chief happened to be a man from Oakham. So, the walls of the Great Hall are covered from top to bottom with horseshoes, ranging from ones only a few inches in diameter to one that is a yard across. Among the earliest that are identifiable is one presented by Elizabeth I; among the latest is one presented by our own Sovereign, Elizabeth II, and as recently as 1967, and one by the Royal Consort, the Duke of Edinburgh. (It will be noticed by the superstitious that all the horseshoes have been hung upside-down, so that 'luck runs out of the points'!) There are horseshoes presented by Queen Victoria, George VI, and Edward VIII while he was still Duke of Windsor; there is an outstanding one of bronze and ormolu presented by George IV when he was Prince Regent. Look for Gibbet Gate, where for centuries the gallows stood, visible from appropriately named Swooning Bridge. Look, too, for the thatched cottage in which, in 1619, Jeffery Hudson, the 'Rutland Dwarf', was born; he was served up in a pie to Charles I. Dominating the little town is the magnificent fourteenth-century spire of the Parish Church of All Saints, the oldest part of which, the South Porch, dates from 1190. Not surprisingly, the motto on Oakham's coat of arms is *Multum in Parvo*.

RICHMOND

This is the North Riding town of the charming eighteenth-century song, 'The Lass of Richmond Hill'. Its history, however, goes back many centuries further than that. This 'town of grey grandeur, gloriously defying time' stands on the bank of the fastest-flowing English river, the Swale, and claims to be the most perfectly sited market town in England. Leland referred to it as a 'Towne that Standith on Unequal Grounde', and quite rightly too. For though parts of it lie low at the approach to the Vale of York, its great ruined Norman castle (upper picture) is built on the sheer edge of a precipitous slope beneath which a loop of the river swirls by. North of the castle, the medieval cobbled Market Place (lower picture) slopes downward, overlooked by Holy Trinity Church. Richmond was made a Royal Borough by Edward III in 1329, and for centuries was the largest corn market in the whole of the north of England. Its mayor has the title of Clerk of the Market, and on Market Day (Saturday) two fifteenth-century halberds are still placed outside the door of his residence.

There is no market hall, as such, in the Market Place; but there is an obelisk 65ft high, first installed in Henry VI's reign though it was rebuilt in 1771, its focal point. A curious fact is that the town's 12,000-gallon reservoir used to lie beneath it. More interesting, and vastly more ancient, however, is Holy Trinity Church, which overlooks it. An unusual feature of this is that there are shops beneath the North Aisle – the only example of the survival of what was a regular practice in this country in the Middle Ages. (It is believed that there were shops in the aisles of the St Paul's Cathedral that was destroyed by the Great Fire of 1666.) There is added interest in the fact that this church, largely destroyed in 1360 and then rebuilt, served also at intervals as a school, a warehouse, and as a refuge during successive plagues; also, the North Aisle was used prior to 1745 as both Consistory Court and Assize Court – again a most unusual circumstance.

From the church tower the nightly *couvre-feu* – the curfew – is rung at eight o'clock; also, at eight o'clock every morning the even more unusual 'Prentice-bell' is rung, a reminder of the days of the medieval guilds, of which there were thirteen in Richmond. On a smaller scale, the town is reminiscent of Durham, with its castle high above the loop of the river, here spanned by a three-arched bridge; but it is more intimately picturesque, every corner and 'wynd' exuding medievalism.

North Yorkshire

RIPON

Strictly speaking, this is a minor cathedral city; indeed, its thirteenth-century Cathedral Church of St Wilfrid, with its remarkable West Front, is one of the most interesting, architecturally, in the country. It stands on the site of an Anglo-Saxon church destroyed a thousand years ago, but its crypt survives and is comparable with the one at Hexham. However, Ripon is essentially a market town. Its two-acre, rectangular Market Square (upper picture) is dominated by a 90ft obelisk, higher by nearly thirty feet than the one in Richmond's Market Place, a memorial to citizen William Aislabie who was the MP for sixty years. In the Middle Ages the town was a cloth-making centre of great importance; more unusual, it was a centre for lace-making, the only one in all Yorkshire. Tradition has it that lace-making was established by a community of refugee nuns, and some monks – a pleasing thought. The craft died out, but there was one solitary lacemaker still at work about a century ago.

There is no market hall, as such, and the Town Hall, overlooking the Market Square, designed in 1801 by William Wyatt, is of no great architectural distinction though it has a certain classic dignity. Look carefully at its façade, however, and you will see, boldly inscribed across it, the town's motto: 'Except Ye Lord Keep Ye Cittie, Ye Wakeman Waketh (watcheth) in Vain.' Incidentally, this motto has been adopted by the sister town of Ripon, Wisconsin, USA. This brings us to what is the most interesting feature of Ripon. In one corner of the Market Square is the Wakeman's House (lower right). It is a fourteenth-century building, for many years the official mayoral residence though now it houses a museum. Prior to 1604 the Wakeman was mayor of the town; today he is so no longer, but is known as the Mayor's Hornblower.

Every night at nine o'clock precisely he makes the circuit of the Market Square, blowing a blast on the magnificent ornamented buffalo horn at each corner and finally opposite the Town Hall. This tradition is known to have been maintained for five hundred years, and possibly for twice as long. It was originally known as 'setting the watch'; the Hornblower (lower left) was then responsible for the welfare of the sleeping inhabitants. In fact, if a citizen was unfortunate enough to have his house burgled during the night, the Hornblower (or Wakeman, as he was then known) had to make good the loss; so, his honourable office was by no means a sinecure.

84

ROSS-ON-WYE

This old market town owes part of its beauty to its setting: on a red sandstone elevation part-circumscribed by a sweep of the incomparably beautiful River Wye. But it owes almost as much to the genius, inspiration and devotion of a local worthy, one John Kyrle, who died in 1724 just short of ninety years old. He had taken the place, as it were, under his wing and lavished upon it his resources and his imagination; not for nothing did he come to be known as 'The Man of Ross', and have his praises sung by Samuel Taylor Coleridge. He was a man of wealth and leisure; one of the noblest buildings in the town is the Elizabethan house in which he lived and died (lower picture). For some years thereafter it was an inn, *The King's Arms*, and it was beneath its roof that Coleridge wrote his 'Ode to the Man of Ross'. Behind it is the ornate Gothic-style summer-house he had built for his own private pleasure.

Standing in the doorway of No 34, you look immediately across the triangular market place at the Market Hall (upper picture), which is hard to surpass anywhere in the country. It is yet another example of a free-standing market house, supported on fourteen stone arches rising from great columns on a massive plinth and consisting in effect of two buildings linked together, with paired windows along their sides and triple windows beneath the gables, the whole topped by a square gabled clock tower with four clock faces beneath the broad eaves and a weather-vane above all. The Market Hall, dated 1670, is the more remarkable in that, like its fellow at Barnard Castle, it stands on a slope.

If the town's chief architectural feature is the Market Hall, built when John Kyrle was still a young man, it has other outstanding features in plenty. The Prospect, for instance: a walled public garden round the ancient Church of St Mary, which was designed by The Man of Ross; the raised causeway which he designed, leading to the sixteenth-century Wilton Bridge; the fourteenth-century church spire, which he renovated when he provided the tower with its pinnacles; the famous row of elm trees that he planted in the churchyard. There, incidentally, is the rare 'Plague Cross', with the inscription on its plinth: 'Plague, Anno. Dom. 1637. Burials 315. Libera Nos, Domine.' About Ross-on-Wye there is an echo of the Cotswolds, though the sandstone of Herefordshire is ruddier than the golden limestone of Gloucestershire. Is there any other town in all England on which one man's imprint is more marked?

Warwickshire

ROYAL LEAMINGTON SPA

Its name singles it out from the category of strictly market towns. Country town: yes indeed; but market town – never! A century and a half ago it was a hamlet of barely six hundred inhabitants; today it is twenty times that size. The reason? The restorative effects of its mineral waters, known as long ago as in Elizabethan times (but, unlike Bath, not in Roman times), for it is mentioned by the Elizabethan antiquarian William Camden, whose comments on the English scene are so discerning. Its resources began to be exploited towards the end of the eighteenth century, when William Abbots built the first Spa Bath there. Even then its full potential was not fully recognised; it had to be 'put on the map', as it were, by Dr Henry Jephson, a physician of the town who there 'received' the young Queen Victoria in 1838.

Not surprisingly, therefore, you will look in vain for the medieval element; indeed, you will look in vain for buildings of the seventeenth and early eighteenth centuries. The great beauty of the architecture of Royal Leamington Spa is to be found in its Regency buildings. Houses in Portland Street (lower picture), with their fine wrought-ironwork, and in Waterloo Place (upper picture), equally distinguished though terraced, are typical of the best to be found in an inland watering-place that received its cachet 'Royal' after Queen Victoria's first visit, and has lived up to its reputation to this day. There is, too, much that emanates from the Victorian Age, but this also is worthy of notice. There is a sense of dignity, if not of true splendour, about the streets, crescents and squares; a sense of spaciousness and the tone of serenity that accompanies this element, so lacking today. Even with new shopping centres and increasing traffic, there is the sense of slipping back a little into a more leisurely age: a welcome experience.

On the north side of the River Leam, crossed by the Victoria Bridge, are mellow Georgian, Regency and Victorian houses; Newbold Terrace, if less distinguished than Lansdowne Crescent, can be compared with some of the best terraces of houses that Bath can offer – no mean praise! The spaciousness is perhaps symbolised by the Gardens, laid out as a memorial to Jephson the physician, but for whom perhaps the township would never have achieved the reputation it possesses today. Here, not yarn or butter, fleece or poultry or cattle are sold; there is no market hall; good health is the commodity in demand, and it is dispensed liberally to those who apply.

SAFFRON WALDEN

Originally known simple as Walden, a thriving cloth-making township whose prosperity is evident from the Church of St Mary, the largest in the county, with a tapering 200ft spire, the word Saffron was added when the cloth industry declined, to be replaced by the unique industry of growing, harvesting and processing saffron. The product of the wild crocus, it was used as a dye and also for medicinal purposes and its cultivation maintained the town's prosperity well into the eighteenth century. (Today, one associates it essentially with the 'saffron buns' of Cornwall.)

The little town dates back to Saxon times, and earlier. In AD 700 a palisade surrounded the area where, in the twelfth century, the Normans built a castle, though little remains today; seven centuries ago, however, it dominated all else from its lofty site. More important, a market town resulted, and evidence of this meets you at every turn. It was well established by the Middle Ages, with its Butchers' Row and Poultry Hill, its Drapers' Row and Mercers' Row and, comprehensively, Market Row. There is probably no other town in all England (not ignoring Ludlow in Shropshire) where the *pattern* of the medieval market system is better exemplified. Though shops have long since replaced the stalls and booths, the fifteenth-century scene can easily be visualised.

The buildings reflect the substantial quality of the townsfolk of those times: half-timbering hard to better even in Hereford and Worcester abounds. One of the finest examples is Myddylton Place (lower picture), with its huge timbers and overhanging upper storey and the unusual and impressive sack hoist projecting above all, though in fact it is an eighteenth-century addition. There are old timbered houses in High Street, in The Close, in Bridge Street and Castle Street and elsewhere in abundance. There are also some fine examples of late-Georgian houses. More unusual, though common in neighbouring Suffolk, is the exterior plaster-work known as 'pargetting'. It is seen at its best on the façade of the *Sun Inn* (upper picture). Slanting sunlight gives it the effect of true bas-relief, but the tone is almost always pure medieval. The most unusual feature in the town – an exceptionally rare one, in fact – is The Maze. It is a true maze, set out in turf and brick, the origins of which quite certainly date back to prehistoric ritual, though only the archaeologist or antiquarian can tell its true story.

SHAFTESBURY

Standing on a 700ft hilltop and so commanding a magnificent view across into Wiltshire, this town is more remarkable for its site and tradition than for its buildings. King Alfred founded an abbey here in about AD 888, appointing his daughter Aethelgiva its first abbess; a century later the martyred King Edward was brought here for burial; little of the ancient Benedictine foundation now remains to be seen.

Perhaps the two most remarkable features of 'Shaston' are Tout Hill and Gold Hill (lower picture). The first is so steep that in stage-coach times four extra horses had to be hitched on to draw coaches to the summit; Thomas Telford himself was commissioned to devise a means of easing the gradient. Up and down this hill ran the historic London-Devonport Mail Coach, stopping daily at 6.30 in the morning at the *Grosvenor Inn*. Gold Hill, cobbled and winding, is even more spectacular: perhaps the most interesting street in any small Dorset town. Its thatched and tiled cottages seem like steps alongside – a glimpse of real old-time Shaston. Because the only wells were located on the lower outskirts of the town, all water had to be carried up these hills; many labourers earned their livelihood carrying buckets of water at one farthing a time or pushing barrow-loads at twopence a time, from bottom to top. Such was the picture well into the seventeenth century and later.

At the top of Gold Hill, behind St Peter's Church (upper picture), is a small museum. It was originally a doss-house for vagrants and for drovers bringing cattle to Shaston Market. Today it offers an interesting record of the life of a Saxon township that sprang up round an old abbey. Other buildings well worth more than a casual glance are the old Fire Engine House at the junction of Bell Street and High Street, with its fire-hooks (for removing burning thatch), old-style ladders and other equipment and implements; Ox House, which is mentioned in Hardy's *Jude the Obscure*; Blind House, on Gold Hill, which five centuries ago was the Town Gaol; the Court Room, behind the *Grosvenor Inn*, where the Quarter Sessions were held until the first half of last century; and of course the Town Hall, where you may see the famous 'Byzant', an ornate and immensely valuable 'Prize Besom' which linked the Mayor and townsfolk with the Lord of the Manor and enabled them, for an annual ritual gesture, to benefit from his private water supply.

SHREWSBURY

'Shrobbesbyri standithe on a rokky hill of stone, and Severne so girdethe-in all the towne that, savinge a little pece it were an isle.' So wrote traveller-historian Leland four centuries ago. With the exception perhaps of Durham, on its cliff top overlooking the Wear, it is the only county town in England looped about by a river. In the fifth century it was the seat of the formidable Princes of Powis; in the eighth century King Offa of Mercia captured it from the Welsh; for centuries thereafter it remained a border town, constantly disputed. It survives as one of the best preserved medieval towns in England, 'crammed with history' in what remains of its encircling walls. Even today, its essential atmosphere is Tudor: street names such as Wyle Cop, Murivance, Milk Street, Shop Latch, Shoemakers Row, Gullet Passage and Grope Lane (lower picture) catch the the spirit of those far-off days; Queen Elizabeth I were she to return, would soon feel at home!

Shrewsbury Castle (upper picture) stood outside the walls. Built in the twelfth century, little now survives apart from one major section of its walls, the postern gate and main gateway: it was too obvious a target for attack to survive complete. The dominant and immediate impact is the spire of the twelfth-century Church of St Mary, one of the three tallest in England; it contrasts strongly with the most unusual Church of St Chad, overlooking the river, which has a rare *circular* nave and is crowned with a tower that consists, unexpectedly, of a dome and a minaret.

Most memorable, however, are the numerous medieval timber-built edifices large and small: the Abbot's House in Butcher Row, for instance, dating from 1450. Here the shops are the original ones, with the broad oaken sills on which the wares were displayed, as in the open-fronted booths of Moroccan and other merchants today. Off almost every one of the narrow, crooked, medieval streets, glimpses may be caught of little alleys, tiny shops, half-hidden courtyards, with overhanging half-timbered façades casting deep shade on cobbles and slabs even at high noon. More open, of course, is the Market Square, with its stone-pillared Market Hall dating from 1596. For this was essentially a merchants' town, and evidence of their prosperity is apparent in their fine half-timbered dwellings 'built on wool and cloth'. Notable among these are Owen's Mansion and Ireland's Mansion. It is not for nothing that Shrewsbury has been dubbed by connoisseurs 'England's finest Tudor town'.

Lincolnshire

STAMFORD

There was a 'stane' (stone) ford across the River Welland on this south-north route at least as far back as Roman times: hence the name; viewed across the river (lower picture) it clearly deserves its reputation as one of the finest and best integrated stone-built towns in England. Providentially, it is now bypassed, for increasing traffic up and down the old Great North Road that runs through it could have destroyed it; now it has reverted to the serenity of centuries, and is a veritable treasurehouse of noble stonework. Because of its site, its history predates the Romans. They in turn were routed here by Queen Boudicca in AD 61. The Danes created it one of their five Danelaw Burghs, capital of Fenland. The Saxon King Edgar granted it the right to mint its own coins, in 972. The Normans built a castle here. By the twelfth century it was already famous for 'Stamford Cloth'. In 1254 Henry III granted it a Royal Charter, and it has flourished ever since. Though its many religious establishments have vanished, there are relics of these, such as Whitefriars Gateway. Everywhere there is evidence of the affluence of the merchants who 'made' Stamford.

Notable among the buildings they sponsored are the many almshouses, above all Browne's Hospital in Broad Street, erected in 1480 to house 'Eleven Poore Men and One Woman'. The almshouses are generally known as 'Callises' – a reminder that the wool men traded with Calais. It is in Broad Street that the famous Open Market, consisting of 120 stalls (upper picture) is held every Friday. Dominating the town at the crest of the main road that climbs from the river is the magnificent fourteenth-century 163ft spire soaring above the thirteenth-century Church of St Mary. Particularly noteworthy inside is the famous Chapel of the Golden Choir, in which gold stars frame a pattern of curious, even grotesque, images.

There are five other notable churches. More unusually, there is a labyrinth of crypts, vaults and subterranean passages that once linked some of the religious houses; some of these can still be explored, among them one below the posting-house, *The George*, with its 'London' and 'York' waiting-rooms used by long-distance stage-coach travellers. The High Street, and other streets, are lined with gracious Regency and Georgian and earlier buildings; Sir Walter Scott termed it 'The finest scene between London and Edinburgh'; architecturally speaking, few would dispute the claim.

96

SWAFFHAM

Many East Anglian townships – Castle Acre in Norfolk and Bungay in Suffolk, for example – have as it were on their doorsteps carved and painted figures not merely carrying their name but objects of beauty and interest in themselves, often 'telling a story'. As good an example as any is the one bearing the name of the 'ham', or settlement, of the Germanic Swaefa tribe that established itself here after the departure of the Romans in the late fourth century. It portrays the Patron Saint of the place – in fact a tinker named Chapman. Beneath the feet of the charming carved image are the words: 'Ye Pedlar of Swaffham Who Did by a Dream Find a Great Treasure.' According to tradition he had dreamed that if he dug deep in a certain spot he would come upon a hoard of gold. He dug, as bidden; the gold was there, as promised, in two buried chests. In gratitude (the legend goes) he built the fine tower and arcaded aisle of the fifteenth-century Church of SS Peter and Paul (both pictures), completing the work in 1510.

Rightly, Chapman is remembered everywhere. In the triangular Market Place, where there is a graceful eighteenth-century Greek temple-like, stone-pillared and domed rotunda (lower picture) with a dignified statue, erected by the then Earl of Oxford, instead of the more usual Market Hall or Cross, there is a monument to him. In the church, with its open-work lantern and needle spire, beyond the Market Place, he may be found, together with his faithful dog, carved on the prayer-desk and elsewhere; brasses, too, portray him and his dog. The church offers the additional attraction in that it rises behind a beautiful stand of deciduous trees – a comparative rarity in a county not rich in trees other than conifers.

The ecclesiastical authorities have cause for gratitude. This church has a magnificent double hammer-beamed roof such as would usually be found only in more important churches, and the main beams are supported by a notable array of angels with open wings. It possesses, too, a remarkable library of some four hundred rare and ancient volumes, housed in a room over the vestry and open to view. Among these is a pre-Reformation 'Terrier' volume, the Black Book of Swaffham. In it is the full story of the Pedlar of Swaffham; and there is a reference to one John Chapman – possibly the pedlar himself – who was a churchwarden here in the fifteenth century when the original church was being reconstructed, much of it at 'The Pedlar's' own expense.

TENTERDEN

There are larger and more important market towns in this county, but not one of them surpasses in beauty and charm what has been called by no less an authority than the authors of the Penguin Guide 'The most delightful country town in Kent'. Superlatives are usually suspect, but – well go and see for yourself!

Its broad High Street (both pictures) runs from East Cross to West Cross; for much of its length it is flanked by the well-known 'greens', a continuous belt of smooth, sloping turf scattered with plane and lime trees, the turf interrupted by stone-flagged tracks leading to shops and houses lying back from the road, almost every one of which merits more than a passing glance. The general impression is of Georgian style, interspersed with white-painted weatherboarding. But very often what appear to be bricks flanked by stone quoins which are in fact known as 'mathematical tiles'. These are brick-shaped tiles suspended flush on a timber framework that is often of medieval origin, the quoins actually being of white-painted wood.

In the Middle Ages the coastline was very different from what it is today: the English Channel flowed into an irregularly shaped estuary and Tenterden stood close to its own port, Smallhythe; the township possessed strategic importance and was therefore linked with the Confederation of the Cinque Ports. After the water receded, Tenterden closed in on itself. Later, it opened its arms to the Huguenot refugees who flocked into it in the fourteenth century, to develop as a recognised centre for woollen manufacture, weaving, and marketing. The present early-nineteenth-century Market Hall replaces the medieval one, which stood near the *White Lion*, one of the little town's many interesting hostelries.

The Parish Church of St Mildred, first built in the twelfth century, has a magnificent 120ft tower from which, in clear weather, the French coast can be seen; at the time of the Armada, the beacon lit on top of it was one of a chain that burned along the whole of the south coast. The tower was built so high to provide a landmark for shipping bound for Smallhythe, on the orders of the Bishop of Rochester, who had 'interests' in the port business! The stonework of the tower is 'Bethersden marble', locally quarried. The church shares a feature with five others in England: twin West Doors. But interesting as this may be, it is Tenterden's quiet charm that most impresses.

TETBURY

Though this is one of the less well-known Cotswold townships, perhaps because it lies far to the south of the better-known ones and almost on the Wiltshire border, it nevertheless deserves more than a casual visit. There was a settlement here on the banks of the upper Avon in prehistoric times, as is proved by the discovery of flint implements dug up locally. Roman coins have been found here, too, and there was a small monastery here in the seventh century. Later, the Normans built a castle, destroyed in Tudor times. Markets have been held here from the fourteenth century onwards, the most important sales being those of the woolstaplers.

The centre of the town is still known, revealingly, as The Chipping, and the mid-seventeenth-century Market House (opposite), known also as the Town Hall, is justifiably scheduled as an Ancient Monument. An exceptionally fine example of a free-standing venue for traders, this great stone building, dated 1665, consists of three rows of massive barrel-shaped pillars, with capitals, supporting a Great Chamber buttressed at the corners, lit by diamond-paned windows with the characteristic Cotswold-style dripstones, the whole topped by a gabled roof. The main face of the building (upper picture) has eight triple windows (one blocked-off), topped by a small gable with a boldly designed clock and the whole surmounted by a charmingly lightweight cupola bearing a weather-vane.

It is from the Great Chamber, where the town's business affairs were long conducted, that one of the best views of Tetbury's centre may be obtained. You look out across the Market Place, or Chipping, and so down the vista of Long Street, with its steeply-gabled buildings, some of them half-timbered, which are carried on a succession of pillars only just less substantial than those of the Market House itself, and reminiscent of those in, for example, parts of Totnes, Devon. By comparison with the Market House, and indeed many of the old stone houses, the Church of St Mary is quite new, dating only from 1781, though there was a church here many centuries earlier. The style is Neo-Gothic, but the tall spire rising from the pinnacled tower was rebuilt a century later. One small detail: a sense of age and long use is experienced from the fact that The Chipping must be approached by stone steps leading up to it, worn smooth by the passage of countless generations of heavy footwear.

THAXTED

Today, only about a quarter the size of neighbouring Saffron Walden, you might call this a village; yet some centuries ago it was a market town of considerable importance, with a population much larger than that of today. The splendid Church of St John the Baptist (upper picture), a landmark for miles in every direction, is evidence of this. Another landmark, incidentally, is the tower mill, built in 1804 to replace one originally built on the same high site, adjoining the church; dedicated windmill lovers are at present engaged on the costly task of rehabilitation.

It has been said that Thaxted 'offers the history of England in miniature'; the Elizabethan antiquary, Camden, described it as 'a little mercate towne seated very pleasantly upon a high rising hill'. It was a Saxon *stead*, or place, where *thaec*, or thatching material, was easily come by: hence its name. Its prosperity derived, not from wool, as in neighbouring Suffolk, or from saffron, as at Saffron Walden, but from the reputation it gained in the mid-fourteenth century for the skill of its cutlers in sharpening and sheathing knives and sword-blades: Cutler's Green, today, is a reminder of this. The fifteenth-century Guildhall (lower picture), of outstanding beauty and timbered dignity, was almost certainly erected by the Guild of Cutlers, whose membership numbered nearly a hundred. It is a three-storeyed, timber-framed and plaster-work building with a roof (restored some two hundred and fifty years ago) hipped in twin spans. As so often in like buildings, the ground floor, built over a spacious cellarage, forms an open-sided, flagged Market House; behind this, a stairway leads to an upper floor and The Cage, or town lock-up; this floor overhangs the lower one, and a third floor overhangs both, so that the whole is a most impressive structure. Thanks to the intelligent care that has been lavished upon it, it remains in magnificent condition. Not surprisingly, as in so many country towns, the administration of the Borough has for long been carried on beneath this roof.

Other outstanding buildings include some typical weavers' houses; the seventeenth-century Beech House, and Clarance House, dating from the next century. There are, again as in so many towns with a long tradition of prosperity and piety combined, almshouses, to be found here in the churchyard; in fact, innumerable unobtrusive cottages bespeak the medieval tradition that is so essential a feature of Thaxted.

TOTNES

This is, to South Devon, what Barnstaple is to North Devon; like Abingdon, in Berkshire, its centre has been pronounced a Conservation Area of Historic Merit. Local tradition has it that the town was founded by the great grandson of Aeneas – nonsense, of course; but it was an Anglo-Saxon stronghold and, like Barnstaple, had its own mint. By the eleventh century it was a Borough; King John granted it a special Charter of Privileges, including the right to have its own Merchant Guild. It was a walled town with three gates, including East Gate (upper picture), where Fore Street becomes High Street. Standing at the highest navigable point on the River Dart, it was both a market centre for the West country cloth industry and a river port for traders.

Narrow Fore Street climbs steeply almost from the river towards the remains of the twelfth-century castle. On the right-hand side is the so-called 'Brutus Stone' on which, traditionally, Aeneas's great-grandson named the place 'Dodonesse' – Totnes. Facing this is a remarkable example of an Elizabethan merchant's house, heavily half-timbered, with overhanging upper storeys. It now houses a museum primarily of local artefacts from prehistoric times onwards and including, surprisingly, a prototype 'computer' invented by a Totnes man, Charles Babbage, well over a century ago. On the opposite side, beyond the 'Brutus Stone', is the lovely Guildhall, dated 1616, the year of Shakespeare's death, notable for its array of columns and their ornamental capitals. It is seen here (lower picture) with a group of figures in Elizabethan attire. The explanation? On Tuesdays during the summer the citizens of Totnes put on these costumes – many of them rich and rare – and go about their business in shops and offices and in the open, maintaining the strong Elizabethan character of the little town; among specialised activities is the serving at Charity Stalls in the age-old Pannier Market, akin to that of Barnstaple but on a much smaller scale. In the evenings, Elizabethan-style music and dancing and other homely jollifications.

Above the fifteenth-century East Gate you can climb on to what remains of the medieval town wall and take the 'Rampart Walk'. It offers a fine panoramic view, including shots of the early-fifteenth-century Parish Church of St Mary, built of the local red sandstone but containing fragments of a Norman church; it possesses a superb stone rood-screen dated 1460, second only to that in Exeter Cathedral itself.

WITNEY

The town's coat of arms consists of a shield displaying a glove and a blanket – typifying its traditional industries; white and blue wavy lines representing the Windrush, on whose banks it stands; and a green background representing the near-by Cotswold pastures on which the sheep providing the raw material for its main industry graze. The centre has three symbols of its nine centuries of busy life (Domesday records that in 1085 it possessed two corn mills operated by the river); by 1277 it had its first 'fulling' or cloth-processing mill; it has been nationally, even internationally, known for its blankets to this day. These are the early-eighteenth-century Blanket Hall, remarkable for its rare one-handed clock in its gable; the eighteenth-century Town Hall built on stone columns so as to form an open arcaded piazza; and, facing this, the unusually interesting Butter Cross (upper picture). This is a seventeenth-century structure consisting of four steeply-pitched gables carrying a clock turret with sundial topped by a weather-vane, beneath which a tiled roof slopes outwards, the whole supported on a dozen stone pillars, with a central pillar girt about by stone steps that were probably the plinth of a much older Market Cross, as at Wymondham in Norfolk and elsewhere, the setting for barter and bargain-making.

A leading Witney blanket maker named Early established his weaving mill here three centuries ago; in 1687 James II visited Witney and accepted 'a Pair of Blankets with Golden Fringes'; in 1765 George III and Queen Charlotte received similar gifts from 'the Blanket Makers of Witney'. In 1667 almost 3,000 people 'from 8 yrs old to decrepit old age' were employed here.

Prosperity in those days resulted in spending money on buildings; Witney, close to the noble limestone of the Cotswolds, is remarkable for the variety of these. They may be modest rows facing lawns (lower picture); or they may be the splendid cruciform Parish Church of St Mary. Parts of this date from the twelfth century, but the great four-pinnacled tower and 156ft broach spire, like the main fabric, date from succeeding centuries. It has a notable seven-light window that reaches to the roof, probably the finest fourteenth-century window in the county. There are memorial brasses to the fifteenth-century Wenham family, blanket makers affluent enough to have their private chapel here, a quiet reminder of what brought prosperity and fame to this busy and picturesque little market town.

WOODBRIDGE

The heyday of this delightful little estuary-sited town is long since past, and it has relapsed easily into something of the quietude it knew in the days when the twelfth-century Augustinian priory was its chief feature. The monks constructed a tide mill (upper picture) on the quayside; unhappily, this, the last of such mills, fell into a bad state of disrepair, but it is now being rehabilitated. The priory was granted a Market Charter and during the Middle Ages, Woodbridge made a name for itself both for its woollen industry and as a port for shipment to the Continent. Its sloping Market Square has long been dominated by its sixteenth-century Shire Hall, to which gables in the Dutch tradition (evidence of the town's contact with the Netherlands) were added in 1700. The arcaded ground floor long served as a covered but open market, and the upper floor as the Corn Exchange; in those days, by law, room had to be left for wagons to pass through. The Great Chamber above is approached by twin flights of wroughtiron-railed steps and serves today as the Magistrates' Court. Set in the ornate Dutch-style gable high above the steps is the clock.

There were formerly other industries than wool. More than one vessel that fought the Spanish Armada was built here; ropes were spun in the ropewalk and sailcloth was woven here; on a more domestic note, hatters and glovers plied their useful trade. Evidence of its prosperity appears in many of the well-built and often elegant houses owned by merchants and maltsters, shippers and shipwrights. The people had the great advantage of the presence of Thomas Seckford, 'Master of the Court of Requests' and in close touch with Elizabeth I; it was he who built the Shire Hall, and endowed the Seckford Almshouses (lower picture), largely rebuilt in the last century.

The fifteenth-century Parish Church of St Mary, with its 108ft west tower, is a notable example of Suffolk flint flush-work, unusually reinforced with octagonal buttresses – one of the county's very many churches built by prosperous and pious merchants and so known as 'Wool' churches. But the town possesses one feature that is unique in all England (save for something on a smaller scale at Soham, Cambridgeshire): this is the enormous timber 'steelyard' projecting from the gable of *Ye Olde Bell and Steelyard Inn* at the top of the steeply-falling New Street. It was used to weigh wagons and their loads of corn or malt or whatever by lifting them bodily off the road and sliding massive weights along the beam.

Acknowledgements

The author and publishers acknowledge with thanks permission to reproduce photographs kindly supplied by the following authorities: The British Tourist Authority: pages 11; 13; 15; 19; 23; 25 (top); 29; 31; 33; 35; 37; 39; 45; 47; 49; 53; 57; 59; 61; (top); 65; 67 (bottom); 71; 75; 77; 79; 81; 83; 89; 91; 93; 95; 99; 103; 105; 107; 109; 111 (lower). Aerofilms Ltd: 63. D. T. Atkinson and the Corporation of Ripon: 85. P. G. Bartlett and the Ludlow & District Tourist Association: 69; Geoffrey Berry and the South Lakeland District Council: 55. Lance Cooper: 111 (bottom). S. Jardine and the Blandford Civic Society: 21. The Borough of Barnstable and R. L. Knight: 17. G. N. Wright and the Urban District Council of Frome: 43. B. E. Nicholson: 61 (bottom). Downing Street Studios: 41. Mike Woolley Photographics: 73. Walbrook Photography Ltd and the Ross-on-Wye Chamber of Commerce: 87. Borough of Bury St Edmunds: 27. Hitchin Museum and Art Gallery: 51. Stamford Mercury: 97. The Borough of Tenterden: 101.